"In these beautifully crafted meditations, we are invited to discern our calling, to pray without ceasing, to be taught by death. But most of all, we are invited to seek the presence of God in our lives and in the world. Martin Copenhaver gently awakens us to God's presence pulsing even through the awkward silences of our prayers and our clumsy attempts to care for one another. Each chapter is a benediction — good words offered in blessing."

— **Stephanie Paulsell**
Harvard Divinity School

"Imagine a long walk with an old friend or an evening around a fireplace with a mentor you have long loved and admired. That's something of what it feels like to read Martin Copenhaver's moving and inspiring meditations in this book. . . . A rare storyteller and a warm, wise guide, Copenhaver makes Christian faith seem real, challenging, enormously heartening, and — best of all — joyful. What a gift to have this book to go back to again and again!"

— **Samuel T. Lloyd III**
Trinity Church Boston

ROOM TO GROW

Meditations on Trying to Live as a Christian

Martin B. Copenhaver

WILLIAM B. EERDMANS PUBLISHING COMPANY
Grand Rapids, Michigan / Cambridge, U.K.

Published 2015 by

Wm. B. Eerdmans Publishing Co.

2140 Oak Industrial Drive N.E., Grand Rapids, Michigan 49505 /
P.O. Box 163, Cambridge CB3 9PU U.K.

Printed in the United States of America

21 20 19 18 17 16 15   7 6 5 4 3 2 1

Library of Congress Cataloging-in-Publication Data

Copenhaver, Martin B., 1954-
Room to grow : meditations on trying to live as a Christian /
Martin B. Copenhaver.

pages   cm

ISBN 978-0-8028-7258-6 (pbk. : alk. paper)
1. Christian life — Meditations.
I. Title.

BV4501.3.C6795 2015
242--dc23

2015022774

www.eerdmans.com

This book is dedicated to Village Church.
Because it takes two to gospel.

CONTENTS

CONTENTS

FOREWORD

IMAGINE THAT YOU ARE A PASTOR. You must plan the funeral for the guy in the parable in Luke 12 who tore down his barns to build bigger barns, and then was surprised by death in the night. You have a conversation with his widow. She tells you what a fine man he was, with such good intentions. He never got around to some of those good intentions, because he always had one more barn to build. You reflect on the conversation and conclude, "Death is a teacher."

This remarkable act of interpretative imagination is done by Martin Copenhaver in the opening meditation in this volume. It is remarkable, but Martin does it regularly. That meditation is typical of the way in which he moves us toward the zinger of the biblical text without our noticing until it takes us by surprise.

Martin is no celebrity preacher. He easily could have been. But he had a different calling: to be a pastor of a local congregation, and he has done that faithfully and effectively for a long time. One can sense in these understated, compelling meditations that he is a pastor who has put his bucket down in a congregation — in his case, an alert assembly with high expectations. One can see the sly ways in which he enters into the life and presence and struggles and choices of his congregation that he himself shares with them. This is a preacher in solidarity!

He is a storyteller. But the stories he tells couldn't be mistaken for "sermon illustrations." Rather, they are stories that surprise us by disclosing a dimension of possibility in real life that we hadn't noticed. Sometimes the stories begin with Scripture. Sometimes they start with Martin's own experience or memory as his own concealed thought is revealed. Sometimes they start with what he has noticed or been told about the folks around him. However they start, by the time they finish, we find that our life has been reimagined before our very eyes. His way of re-narrating our life is gentle and done in small bits. What comes through in a cumulative way, however, is the sense that the life we are living need not be the one we continue to live. There is another way; there is another story to perform and tell through our lives. It is a story of grace and risk and neighborliness and generosity. Wise as he is, Martin is never didactic or coercive or capable of reprimand, precisely because he expects his listeners to understand and to care about what he's talking about, and to do some of the work themselves.

Thus he can imagine, for example, that he can hear what he calls "the choir practice" when Paul and his companions are in jail in the book of Acts. He notices that they don't rant or protest; they sing. That ancient report suggests to Martin that it is the work of our lives to locate and identify a song that is deep enough and large enough to be worth singing in the hard places of life. This cannot be a superficial pop song. It must be a song of deep love grounded beyond ourselves. By the time he finishes this act of uncommon imagination, we ourselves can hear something of the ancient jail cadences of gospel freedom. Better than that, we are ready to join the choir in the awareness that the "old, old story" often becomes the "new, new song."

Now this quintessential pastor/preacher has been appointed president of a historic seminary. No one knows yet if he can raise all the money that he will be required to raise. No one knows yet if he will lead his school to a curriculum appropriate to our new, bewildering moment in God's history. But all at the seminary will know that this preacher invites them to reimagine their lives and their school according to the true narrative of God's uncompromising purpose for us. We readers will come to know the same — with gratitude and appreciation — in these meditations.

Walter Brueggemann
Columbia Theological Seminary

PREFACE

AS A BOY, WHEN I WENT SHOPPING for clothes with my mother, she would always ask me to try on items that were about a size too large to fit me perfectly. If the shoe-sizing contraption indicated that I was a size 4, she would ask the store clerk to bring a size 5 for me to try on. If the jeans I tried on were a bit long, she considered them just right because they left me "room to grow." Until I grew into them, I could fold over the pant legs at the bottom, creating a makeshift cuff — not much of a fashion statement, to be sure, but at least that way I wouldn't need another pair of jeans quite so soon.

Wearing clothes that don't fit perfectly can make you look and feel foolish at times, but it also makes a statement to the world that you intend and expect to continue growing. It's not a fashion statement. It's an aspirational statement.

That is how I understand the Apostle Paul's admonition to the Romans: "Put on the Lord Jesus Christ" (NRSV), also translated as "Dress yourself with the Lord Jesus Christ" (CEB). Paul is asking the Romans to assume some of the qualities of Christ, to wear them as they would a new set of clothes.

That's quite a charge. I don't know if the Romans felt up to it. What I do know is that when I try Jesus on for size and look in the mirror, sometimes I can get quite discouraged. When I dress myself with Jesus, I can feel like that boy who's trying to wear an outfit that's at least a size too large. Or, perhaps even more, I can feel like a boy in the attic trying on my father's clothes. Not only do I feel awkward; I can even look a bit silly.

Then I remember my mother insisting that, when trying on a new outfit, it's very important to leave "room to grow." What seems to cause me to trip all over myself today allows for the possibility of growth. And when I clothe myself with Jesus, he leaves me room to grow — which is a good thing because, God knows, I'm still growing. I put on Jesus as I would a new and ill-fitting outfit — in order that someday it might fit and be a fitting expression of who I have become.

The meditations that follow are about ways we can grow in the Christian faith — or, better yet, grow into the Christian faith. I hope that, in their own way, they leave you room to grow and in some way inspire your own growth as well.

These meditations were first offered at Wellesley Congregational (Village) Church, United Church of Christ, a remarkable congregation I was honored to serve for twenty years. All preaching is dialogical. In these meditations you hear only one side of the dialogue, so I want to testify here that I was blessed to have a wonderful dialogue partner. These meditations were enriched immeasurably by the congregation of Village Church. This book is dedicated to them. How could it be otherwise?

BUILDING BARNS, POSTPONING LIFE

Luke 12:16-21

REMEMBER OR IMAGINE A TIME when someone precious to you has recently died. You're at a social gathering, and you're determined not to talk about your loss. Instead, you resolve, as much as possible, to bob about on the surface of pleasantries along with everyone else. Nevertheless, try as you might, you find it difficult to keep the conversations in focus. Someone is talking about his teenage daughter, who hasn't picked up her room in weeks, and he wonders if she'll ever learn responsibility. In another cluster of conversation, someone else is going on about how crowded the roads are these days and rails against the inability of various levels of government to do anything about it. Then, somehow, the subject turns to real estate taxes: Can they possibly keep going up?

There were other days, other gatherings, when you would have joined in such conversations, but not this time. Instead, you keep seeing the face of that person who is now gone. You ask yourself: *How could they possibly think that any of this really matters?*

Now remember or imagine a time when worries nag you into distraction. The day after you finish paying for the car, you get into a fender-bender, and who knows how much it will cost? Or your son's grades at college are getting worse, and he doesn't seem to appreciate that D's are as expensive as A's. Or you've just begun to make a list of things that must be done tomorrow, and you're already on your second page. Or your boss asks to see you first thing in the morning, and he's never done that before. You toss and turn in your bed, as if wrestling with your worry, and it's a match you're losing. Sleep seems ever more elusive. And then the phone rings, with that urgent, menacing ring that phones seem to reserve for the middle of the night. On the other end is a familiar voice, obviously shaken, telling you that one you have loved has died suddenly that very night — without pain, thank goodness, but gone now nonetheless. And in that instant, whatever it is that was worrying you flies into the night and disappears. It no longer matters.

Death is a teacher. It can teach us many things, silently, by its very presence. When death intrudes, it can give instant perspective to our lives. It helps us sort out what is truly important and what is not. The smaller concerns that so often crowd our hearts and minds can simply scurry away in the presence of death. It is then that we're prepared to see with rare clarity what it is that deserves our attention, our devotion, and our time.

Jesus tells a parable about a farmer who spends his life building one barn after another, each larger than the last, to contain his ever-larger crops of grain (Luke 12:16-21). The farmer promises himself that, when he has accumulated enough, he will cease all that striving, kick back, and "eat, drink, be merry." But before he can do that, God says, "Fool! This very night your soul is required of you."

I try to imagine what it would be like to pay a pastoral call on the widow of the farmer in Jesus' parable. That in itself isn't too difficult because I've made many such calls.

The farmer has just died. His wife is in shock. She asks,

"What is a person to do now? No one has told me what happens next." Her talk wanders, and I follow, mostly just listening. Then we turn to the memorial service, and I ask a few questions about the man who has recently died. You see, I didn't know him too well, although, on those rare occasions when I did see him for a moment or two, I genuinely liked him. But now, as we anticipate a memorial service, I know it's up to me to speak of him as a whole person, not just of those few, fleeting moments I shared with him.

So I ask, "What was important to him?" His widow answers, "His family is — was — very important to him. He was very proud of his children, although I'm not sure they really know how much. His wallet was thick with their pictures. And when we were younger, we used to love taking walks on the beach together. We talked about retiring to the shore so we could take walks like that again. And his church was very important to him, although I know you haven't seen much evidence of that in recent years. He didn't stop believing in God, I'm sure of that, but, somehow, life just got so busy."

I ask, "How did he spend his time?" She replies, "Oh, working on the farm. And he was very successful. We had another bumper crop this year. He didn't want to sell it all at once because if he flooded the markets, the price was sure to fall. So he tore down the barns we had and built larger ones to store the crops. It was a huge task that demanded his full attention. He said he even dreamed about it. It was a lot of pressure.

"As for other parts of his life, well, they were put on hold for a while. It didn't always make things easier for him, either. I would frequently ask him when it would all end and we could get on with our lives. And he would always try to reassure me, mostly by using words like *tomorrow* or *soon* and phrases like *This won't last forever* and *Someday* and *I promise*. And he meant it. I know he did. He often promised me and himself that as soon as he finished his work and gathered all of his goods together, he could say to himself, 'You now have plenty of goods laid up for many years; now you can go to that house on the shore, take your ease, eat, drink, be merry, and do all those things you always talked about.' And now? . . ." She pauses and then seems grateful to be able to change the subject: "Well, let's get back to planning the memorial service. . . ."

Death is a teacher, and among the things it can teach us is the wide and often tragic gap between the questions "What is important to you?" and "How do you spend your time?" Experiencing the death of a loved one or pondering our own death can provide perspective on our lives and help us see what is truly important and worthy of our devotion and what is not.

I believe the farmer when he says he intends to lead a different life someday soon, just as I believe myself when I express similar intentions. Someday soon I really will stay in close touch with friends. Someday soon I will adhere to a more complete and consistent prayer discipline. Someday soon I will give my family the time they deserve. Someday soon I will give a more substantial portion of my time to those who are without food or shelter. And yes, someday soon I will eat, drink, and be merry, too — as soon as the barn is built, as soon as the bills are paid, as soon as I'm a bit more comfortable with my financial situation, as soon as I have fewer obligations, as soon as things slow down, as soon as . . . well, as soon as things are different.

And I feel quite sure that the farmer and I are not alone in this tendency. I've heard so many people speak of how their lives are going to change as soon as their barns are built . . . when they retire, when the children are grown, when the semester is over, when the economy changes, when the task is complete, when the work is done. It's not that we're incapable of doing what we want or should do. It's simply that often we seem incapable of doing those things

4

now. Time is short, and everything else seems so long. And then, in the words of poet Dylan Thomas, "like a running grave, time tracks you down."

In the last decade or so of my father's life, he developed an interest in wine. There is more to this hobby than you might imagine. He would read about the many varieties and vintages and vineyards. He would scout out bargains by reading the newspaper ads from wine shops. When he purchased a wine, he carefully stored and cataloged it. Occasionally he would even drink the stuff. That was always an elaborate ceremony, beginning with bringing the wine to the proper temperature, uncorking it at just the right moment, smelling the cork, taking in the color, tasting the wine to make sure it was suitable to serve, the ritual accompanied by florid commentary about bouquet and body, descriptions that no one else understood or, frankly, cared much about.

When friends learned of my father's interest in wine, they would sometimes give him a special gift of a rare and costly bottle. I never remember those wines being served. He always said he was waiting for a special occasion. But the occasion never came. When my father died quite suddenly — "this very night your soul is required of you" — those bottles remained unopened. I believe he intended to drink them and, oh, how he would have enjoyed the ceremony of it all. But special occasions, like tomorrow, seem never to arrive. As playwright Ben Hecht once put it, "Time is a circus, always packing up and moving away."

Of course, the point here is not that we should eat, drink, and be merry while we have a chance, even as that is not the point of Jesus' parable. The point is that if we postpone the little pleasures at our peril, how much more perilous is our tendency to put off doing what is truly important and noble in life. It may be a good idea to save money for a rainy day, but we sometimes act as if we're saving our lives for a rainy day, and what is most worth doing remains bottled in some dark corner, waiting for that rainy day, or at least another day.

Which brings me to one of the crowning ironies of our lives: The most important things in life are also the most easily postponed. It seems to us that we cannot long postpone building that barn, doing the laundry, running errands, paying the bills. Still, all of those things together don't add up to much of a life. But developing a depth of relationship with one another, taking time for a person in need, learning to pray, growing in relationship with God — all of those things can be postponed, put off until tomorrow.

We may know what's important in life; we may even make room for it . . . tomorrow. And so the future becomes the repository of our noblest impulses. It is to the future that we assign, in the Apostle Paul's words, "Whatever is true, whatever is honorable, whatever is just, whatever is pure, whatever is gracious . . . [whatever is] worthy of praise" (Phil. 4:8).

Years ago now I saw a television program in which David Frost, the British television personality, interviewed several prominent public figures. I don't remember much about that program, what was said, or even who was interviewed. But I do remember one question Frost asked each person. The question was this: "What would you like to have appear in your epitaph?" He could have put the question this way: "On that night your soul is required of you, what would you want to have said about you?" It was a brilliant question because it led each person to consider what was most important to them, what they were living for. And it seemed to catch them off-guard to be, in their imaginations, in the sudden presence of death. Gone were the well-rehearsed statements that had been smoothed like pebbles on a beach through countless interviews. And I remember that the question prompted remarkably similar answers from each of Frost's guests. Each spoke in grand terms about love and bettering the lives of others and even about serving and glorifying God.

I didn't find myself cynical about their responses. I believed them. I believed they desired and intended these things for their lives. And yet, here is that irony again — the irony that the most important things in life are also the most easily postponed. For I doubt very much that the day after the interview, when their aides asked what was on the day's agenda, any responded, "Well, today I think I must better the lives of others and make time to serve and glorify God."

More likely, facing everyday tasks when the teacher death seemed distant again, they probably saved such aspirations for another day so they could focus on how to get re-elected or how to advance their careers or how to make more money — all those present and consuming concerns, all those barns to build.

Jesus does not need to tell us, but we need to be reminded, again and again, that our lives were made for more. Not tomorrow, because we cannot live tomorrow, try as we might. Rather, the only day we have been given — that is, today — was made for more. Certainly we don't want to share the fate of the one who was given the famous epitaph "Born a man, died a grocer," just as we wouldn't want any variation on that theme, such as "Born a man, died with his barns completed." Or "Born a woman, died a politician." Or "Born a man, died a good provider." Or "Born a woman, died with closets clean." It makes us shudder to think that our lives could be so summarized.

Death is a teacher, and from it I think we can learn important lessons. We will learn to tend to the little things today. We will savor the little things with grateful appreciation: a walk on the beach, the taste of wine, the blazing grand finale of color in the leaves of autumn, the embracing stillness of a place apart or another sanctuary for our soul.

And if, in the presence of death, we are led to ponder the end and purpose of life, we will also tend to the big things today. We will not postpone the healing of our relationships with one another or the deepening of our relationship with God. We will listen and care and pray and serve.

It matters what we do with what we have been given. It is the stewardship of our lives — and Jesus injects a sense of urgency about it in this parable. "Don't postpone living" is what I hear Jesus saying. Don't even try to postpone living. Live abundantly. Live now.

Finally, in the end, if we have tended faithfully to the little things and the big things, on that night when our souls are required of us, we will discover that we did not build all the barns we could have, but, with God's help, we did build an abundant life.

PRAY CONSTANTLY

1 Thessalonians 5:12-28

SOON AFTER WHAT WE REFER to in our family as my "unfortunate little episode" — a brief hospital stay to treat a racing and irregular heartbeat — I went to see my doctor for a follow-up exam.

After checking my blood pressure and that sort of thing, he spent quite a bit of time going over the records that were sent from the hospital. Without looking up from those records he asked me questions about my eating, drinking, and exercise habits, which I rather awkwardly answered, knowing that my answers were not in every instance what he would want to hear. Then he asked if I experienced any stress in my life, and I said something like "Well, sure." I wanted to add, "Doesn't everyone?" He expressed some surprise that someone who, in his words, "spends his days caring for souls" could experience anything like stress.

Then he closed my file, and for the first time he looked me straight in the eye and said, "Here's the most important question: Are you praying?" Finally there was a question I could answer without feeling self-conscious or inadequate. "Why, yes, I pray every day." But then came his follow-up question: "Half an hour every day, uninterrupted, no distractions?" "Uh . . . well, uh . . . hmmm . . . not exactly. Not every day, at least." Without

9

shifting his gaze a bit — he wasn't about to give me any wiggle room — he went on to say, "It's the most important thing. For some people I might suggest meditation, but for you it's prayer." My first thought was, *This isn't the prescription I'm used to getting from a doctor.* But then I thought, *Half an hour a day, uninterrupted, no distractions? Does he have any idea what my life is like?*

I used to love to quote the spiritual advisor who said that we should each spend half an hour a day in prayer, with this exception: if the day is really jam-packed with too many things to do, then half an hour is unrealistic. On such days it should be a full hour devoted to prayer. But now my doctor was saying something like that to me. *Hey, that's supposed to be my line!* That was what I thought. What I said was, "I'll try." And I have, with some success. Some. But my life is messy much of the time. It doesn't stay in neat compartments, at least not for long. I have my plans and my intentions, but then life, in all its messiness, intervenes.

If half an hour a day for prayer, uninterrupted, no distractions, sounds hard to pull off, what are we to make of Paul's exhortation to the Thessalonians that we are to "pray continually"? Or, as other translations have it, "Pray without ceasing" and "Pray constantly." Pray all the time. Put in that way, the challenge suddenly becomes more than trying to fit prayer into our lives. The challenge becomes trying to conform our lives to a spirit of prayer.

In order to pray without ceasing, it's not enough to set aside time to pray. Clearly, Paul had something else in mind. If we are to pray constantly, we have to make prayer something more than an isolated activity. We have to weave it into the fabric of our lives. But how do we do that?

I once wrote a book in which the chapter on prayer was entitled "Conversing with God." At the time, that's how I thought of prayer. But now I think that's too narrow a definition. Talking with God is part of what prayer is, as is listening to God — both talking and listening are parts of conversation, and both are parts of prayer — but there is also silent prayer and meditative prayer.

So I now think of prayer more broadly as consciously spending time with God. Obviously, we are in God's presence every moment of our lives, but much of the time we're focused on other things — we're not consciously relating to God. Prayer, then, is what happens when we come alive to God's presence. Through prayer we are not only in God's presence — we know that we are. So prayer is consciously spending time with God, consciously relating to God. It may involve talking and listening, as you do in conversation, or it may involve just being aware that God is with you, like taking a walk with God, neither of you saying a word, just enjoying one another's company.

That's not where you begin, of course. Prayer begins, as most relationships do, perhaps with a bit of shyness and almost certainly with a measure of self-consciousness. Someone once told me about how she was making some initial, tentative gestures toward God in her life. Saying a prayer seemed like too big a step, and she didn't feel ready for it. So, instead, at various points during her day, she would pause and say, "Hello," and then quickly go back to what she was doing. Just that — a shy little "Hello," nothing more. When she told me that, I thought, *Well, that's how a lot of relationships start.* Anything more can be too much at the beginning.

You know how it is when you first meet someone. It's just not as relaxed as seeing someone you know well. There are more conventions about what happens in a conversation between people who don't know each other well than, say, a conversation between close friends. You say certain expected things like "Good to meet you," and you do certain things like try to follow your father's often-repeated advice to always look someone in the eye when you shake his or her hand. So there's a certain self-consciousness about relating to someone you don't know well. You're careful about what you say. You don't want to say the wrong thing. You want to put your best foot forward, make a good impression. So you weigh your words. And then there's the silence! If you don't know some-one well and there's silence in the conversation, it's awkward, to say the least. The silence feels like an emptiness that needs to be filled, and you'll say just about anything to fill it.

Contrast that with spending time with a dear friend who knows you well, perhaps in some ways better than you know yourself, a friend who, after all these years, knows all of your back stories and all of your secrets, who has seen you at your best and at your worst, who knows your weaknesses as well as your strengths, who was there with you in times of joy and in times of despair, the one from whom you cannot hide how you really feel, because this friend knows you so well and can read you like an open book.

Conversations with a friend like that aren't self-conscious. They won't follow any established conventions, except perhaps those that you've established yourselves over the years. With a friend like that, you have different kinds of conversations. Some will be long, heart-to-heart conversations — that is, after all, how you got to be such good friends — but other conver-sations between the two of you will be on the run. Perhaps you'll use just a few sentences to check in, almost in a kind of shorthand, or perhaps you'll use incomplete sentences because the friend knows you well enough to know how you would complete them. And those fragments of conversations on the run can nurture a relationship. It's not all about long heart-to-heart talks. But if it's been a while since you last had an extended conversation in which you were able to go deeper, beyond the day-to-day, to the places in your heart and mind that you would share only with your friend, you'll say, "We need to spend some good uninterrupted time together — no distractions." And during this time there may be silence. But silence between dear friends is different from the silence shared by those who don't know one another well. Silence between dear friends isn't awkward, but in its own way can be savored, as you enjoy the satisfactions of just being together, a companionship beyond the need of words, at least for a time.

A similar dynamic is at work in relating to God in prayer. In the beginning, there's a certain self-consciousness about it. There are conventions you follow, even a kind of formality. You say certain things like "Dear God," and you do certain things like bow your head. You're careful about what you say. You weigh your words. The silences feel empty. And that's okay. That's what happens in the early stages of a relationship.

But if the relationship is nurtured, all of that begins to change. Prayer becomes more like spending time with a dear friend who knows you well. You interact in all kinds of ways. The relationship isn't measured or self-conscious, and the more formal conventions just seem to fall away because they're no longer needed. Many words are shared, but many things can go unsaid because they're simply understood. François Fénelon, a French Christian author of the early eighteenth century, put it this way:

> If you pour out to God all your weaknesses, needs, troubles, there will be no lack of what to say; you will never exhaust the subject; it is continually being renewed. People who have no secrets from each other never want subjects of conversation; they do not weigh their words, because there is nothing to be kept back. Neither do they seek for something to say; they talk together out of the abundance of their heart — without consideration, just whatever they think.[1]

1. François Fénelon, *The Spiritual Letters of Archbishop Fénelon* (London: Rivington, 1877), pp. 205-6.

Prayer approached in this way, as spending time with someone who knows you so well, frees you from the notion that every word must be carefully weighed. God isn't concerned with the words you use. You can let participles dangle and leave sentences incomplete because God knows you well enough to know how to complete them. Or, sometimes, if you use the language of the heart, you may even abandon words entirely and instead merely open your heart and invite God to take a tour of all that resides there — the half-formed thoughts, the elusive longings, the inescapable yet indefinable sense of need. And silence, instead of an emptiness that begs to be filled, can itself be deep and rich, something to be savored, and words just don't seem necessary.

If you have nurtured that kind of relationship with God, prayer can take as many forms as there are ways to relate to a friend — sometimes in long, heart-to-heart conversations and other times in incomplete sentences that sound like shorthand. And that's how you begin to do something like pray constantly.

You wake up in the morning and, with God, you think about what awaits you in the day ahead. You pre-live the day as a kind of prayer. At the breakfast table, you open up the newspaper — another day of horrific stories of violence and disaster — and, as you read, you simply think, *God, be in that place, be with those people.* You get in your car and the traffic is terrible, so you say to God, "The traffic . . . ," and you don't need to say any more because God knows how that sentence ends — "and traffic always makes me tense, because I'll be late for work and I hate to be late, and I have a hard time not taking out my frustration on the first person I meet when I get there." When you arrive, there's a message from your mother. She sounds more confused than ever, so before you pick up the phone you say to yourself, *God, you've got to help me here.* And on like that through the day.

Former President Jimmy Carter once estimated that he prays a hundred times a day. These are the kinds of prayers he was referring to, very few uttered with his eyes closed, perhaps very few that begin with "Dear God" and end with "Amen." Rather, I imagine that his prayers are more seamlessly woven into his life, like spending time with a friend who knows him so well. In fact, his life and his prayers are so interwoven that you cannot separate the two, which I think is what Paul had in mind when he told the Thessalonians, "Pray constantly."

Then, if you are Jimmy Carter, or someone else who has that kind of relationship with God, at the end of a full, messy day, with many distractions, and a hundred short prayers, you give a deep sigh and say to God, "Really, we must find time to get together for a deep heart-to-heart." And in reply, God says, "Thirty minutes, uninterrupted, no distractions?"

EXCUSES, EXCUSES, EXCUSES

Genesis 3:1-13

E ARLY IN OUR MARRIAGE MY WIFE, Karen, and I got tickets to see *The Elephant Man,* which at the time was the hottest show on Broadway. I got those tickets months in advance, and they were good seats, too. I love tickets. I'm a very future-oriented person, so to me tickets are much more than little pieces of cardstock — they are potent little talismans of anticipation. And, because this was to be a special evening, I also got reservations at the best restaurant in the vicinity of the theater.

When the long-anticipated day arrived, my wife and I went out to dinner first. After the main course and before dessert arrived, I took the tickets out of my pocket. I'm with Charlie Brown, who said, "Happiness is holding the tickets in your hand." But as I looked at them, my face went ashen, enough to prompt Karen to ask, "Are you all right? What's wrong?" Well, they were very good seats, as I said, but the tickets were for Tuesday night, and this was Wednesday. We were a day late.

After apologizing to Karen, who was much more understanding than I would have been under the circumstances, I tried to reassure her. "Oh, theaters always have extra seats, even when they say they're sold out. They'll figure something out. I mean, this is a really unusual circumstance. I'm sure they'll understand our predicament and we'll get in." So we skipped dessert, quickly paid the bill, and headed over to the theater. I showed the tickets to the ticket-taker at the door and told him the story of how we ended up with tickets for the wrong night — or, at least, I started to tell the story. Before I could get very far, however, he pointed to a corner of the lobby and said, "Wait over here for Miss Morris."

That response seemed promising, and it gave me a bit of time to think about how best to explain our situation to Miss Morris when she arrived. I would tell her that we had the tickets for months. I would assure her that I had never done anything like this before, that I was actually a very responsible person. And I might even throw in the detail about my being a minister to see if that would help. (I know that's kind of cheesy, but desperate circumstances call for desperate measures.) When I had assembled all of my unique excuses, we simply waited for Miss Morris.

After a few minutes passed, I saw the ticket-taker talking to another couple and then pointing to the corner where my wife and I were standing. The couple came over and stood by us, acting rather anxious. In the next several minutes we were joined by another pair, and then another. Needless to say, their presence made me uneasy. Tentatively, we began to share our stories. One couple was from out of state and had left their tickets at home. A woman said she had picked up the wrong purse when she left her house. Two folks had an excuse very similar to mine — they hadn't noticed that their tickets were for the matinee performance that day and not the evening performance. French filmmaker Jean Renoir observed that we live in a time when "Everyone has his reasons." And, to be sure, in that corner of the lobby, everyone had his or her reasons. In one another's company, however, the power of our excuses faded quickly. They no longer seemed compelling or unique. They became rather embarrassing, actually.

Eventually Miss Morris came over to our little group, patiently heard our stories, or some abridged version of them, and let us in the theater — for standing room. That, I learned, is where excuse-givers are sent — not to hell, perhaps, but to standing room.

I wonder how many excuses the omnipotent Miss Morris hears every day — our unique excuses, repeated over and over again. And if Miss Morris hears a lot of excuses, I wonder how many excuses God hears every day.

In his book *Teacher Man*, Frank McCourt, the Irish author of several wonderful memoirs, tells of his experience teaching English at a rough-and-tumble public high school in Staten Island. After he had been at the school for a time, he began to collect the notes he received from students excusing their absence or their inability to complete an assignment. Those notes supposedly were from a parent, but they were clearly forged. Nothing particularly noteworthy in that.

What interested McCourt, however, and prompted him to save the excuse notes was how wonderfully written they were. They were far superior to any other writing his students had done. "If [their parents] could read those notes," he wrote, "they'd discover their kids capable of the finest American prose: fluent, imaginative, clear, dramatic, fantastic, focused, persuasive, useful."[1]

"The stove caught fire and the wallpaper went up and the fire department kept us out of the house all night."

"Arnold doesn't have his work today because he was getting off the train yesterday and the door closed on his school bag and the train took it away. He yelled to the conductor who said very vulgar things as the train drove away. Something should be done."

1. Frank McCourt, *Teacher Man* (New York: Scribner, 2005), p. 84.

"A man died in the bathtub upstairs and it overflowed and messed up all Roberta's homework on the table."

"Her big brother got mad at her and threw her essay out the window and it flew away all over Staten Island which is not a good thing because people will read it and get the wrong impression unless they read the ending which explains everything."

"We were evicted from our apartment and the mean sheriff said if my son kept yelling for his notebook he'd have us all arrested."

McCourt reflected, "Isn't it remarkable . . . how they resist any kind of writing assignment in class or at home. They whine and say they're busy and it's hard putting two hundred words together on any subject. Why? I have a drawer full of excuse notes that could be turned into an anthology of Great American Excuses."[2]

So one day he gave his students an assignment. He wrote on the board "An Excuse Note from Adam to God" and "An Excuse Note from Eve to God." He told his students that they could start their essays in class and finish them at home. Their response was remarkable: "The heads went down. Pens raced across paper. They could do this with one hand tied behind their backs. . . . The bell rang, and for the first time in my three and a half years of teaching, I saw high school students so immersed they had to be urged out of the room by friends hungry for lunch."[3]

That assignment prompted the most imaginative and expressive writing he had seen from his students. They came up with some brilliant excuses for Adam and Eve.

I wonder how many excuses Frank McCourt heard during his tenure at that school? He said he had a desk drawer full of

2. McCourt, *Teacher Man*, pp. 85-86.
3. McCourt, *Teacher Man*, p. 87.

excuse notes. I wonder how big that drawer was. And if that drawer was big, I wonder how big the drawer is that God must have to hold all of our excuses.

We humans wasted no time before making excuses for our behavior. According to the biblical account, among the very first words spoken by a man or a woman were words of excuse. God asked Adam, "Have you eaten from the tree of which I commanded you not to eat?" Adam responded, "The woman whom you gave to be with me, she gave me the fruit of the tree, and I ate." God then turned to Eve: "What is it you have done?" Eve replied, "The serpent tricked me, and I ate."

But it doesn't end there. The Bible is full of excuses. Could it be any other way? After all, human life is full of excuses. So when God addresses Moses from the burning bush, calling him to lead the people of Israel out of exile in Egypt, Moses immediately begins to offer excuses why he cannot. He tries one excuse after another. First, Moses says, in essence, "Why me? I'm not the right person for this job." When God addresses that excuse, Moses goes on to the next one: "I don't have any authority." When God assures Moses that he will go with God's own authority, he says, "The people won't believe that you sent me." "I will give you a sign," God replies. Moses comes back with, "But I have a bad stutter. And it's worse when I'm nervous. Who's going to listen to me?" The Lord, who between the time of Adam and the time of Moses has already heard every excuse in the book, responds, "Your brother Aaron can speak for you." Finally out of excuses, Moses is reduced to pleading, "Oh please, send someone else." Moses could have used Aldous Huxley's advice: "Several excuses are always less convincing than one."

Then, later in the book of Exodus, Moses is on the receiving end of excuses. When he comes down from Mount Sinai after God has given him the Ten Commandments, he finds the people dancing around a statue of a golden calf in an act of worship. Moses, who left his brother Aaron in charge, confronts him. Aaron immediately starts to make excuses: "You know the people. They are bent on evil. They said to me, 'Make us gods, who shall go before us; as for this Moses, the man who brought us up out of the land of Egypt, we do not know what has become of him.' So I said to them, 'Whoever has gold, take it off'; so they gave it to me, and I threw it into the fire, and out came this calf!" (Exod. 32:22b-24). Notice: It's the people's fault! It's your fault, Moses! It's the calf's fault! (Out came this calf? Out of its own volition?) Huxley was right: Several excuses are always less convincing than one.

In one of Jesus' parables he compares the Kingdom of God to a great banquet. A broad invitation is sent out, but many give excuses for why they cannot attend: "I've just bought some real estate and I must tend to it; please accept my regrets." "I've just bought some new farm equipment — two oxen — and I want to take them for a spin." "I just got married. I'll be on my honeymoon." And here's the painful part of that parable: those who offer excuses miss out. We might think that the excuses are good ones, but even good excuses can prevent those who offer them from experiencing the greatest blessing of all.

Excuses have no place in the Christian life. As Christians, we don't have to make excuses. In fact, it is something like a lack of faith to offer them. After all, we can't justify ourselves. That is God's job. We are, in Paul's wonderful phrase, "justified by grace through faith." There's another way to put this: We are free to recognize that we are not perfect people. We can do that because we rely on the perfect love of God. So the Christian alternatives to excuses are confession and forgiveness.

Sometimes I'm tempted to throw some excuses in with my confessions. "God, here's what I did and I'm really sorry, but let me tell you why I did that. I had my reasons. Everyone has his reasons." But that isn't really a confession, is it? Author Kimberly Johnson advises, "Never ruin an apology with an excuse." That's good advice that applies to confession as well: "Never ruin a confession with an excuse." We can afford to follow that advice because we rely on the forgiveness of God.

How big is that drawer where God keeps our excuse notes? It must be really big. But this is also true: it's not as big as God's capacity for forgiveness.

The other alternative to making excuses is to practice forgiveness with one another. What if we were the kind of community that regularly, consistently offered forgiveness to one another? That is, after all, the kind of life we are called to live. We are regularly to forgive one another in the name of the God who continually, consistently forgives us all. And if we do, there's no longer a need for excuses.

We expect that in the world it will be excuses, excuses, excuses. And sometimes it will be that way among us as well. After all, such habits are hard to break. But what if we really believed in the forgiveness of God and could rely on the forgiveness of one another?

What if, instead of excuses, excuses, excuses, we heard forgiveness, forgiveness, forgiveness?

AN EVERLASTING SONG TO AN EVER-PRESENT GOD

Psalm 23

THE TWENTY-THIRD PSALM is among the most familiar passages in all of Scripture. It is beloved by Jews, Christians, and wistful agnostics. Henry Ward Beecher called this the "nightingale" of the Psalms. And, indeed, its musical cadences have rippled through the lives of countless people since childhood.

These are the first verses of Scripture I ever memorized. In a way it's odd that we would teach this psalm to children because it speaks of realities that a child has yet to confront fully — "the shadow of death" (or, if you prefer, "the darkest valley"), evil, and enemies. A child may know something about these things, because in our world they are almost as ever-present as the God whom the psalm praises. But when most children learn this psalm, they have yet to encounter fully the realities of which it speaks: the ever-grasping greediness of death, the isolating threat of darkness, the stony grip of evil, and the lingering corrosiveness of enemies. So, although this psalm may speak to all of us, it takes a lot of living for its depths to resonate in our hearts. Eventually, however, in one way or another, life gives each of us reason to long for a companion who, in Robert Frost's phrase, is "acquainted with the night." For many, this psalm is just such a companion.

When we teach children this psalm, then, I think that we're giving them a gift that may take them a lifetime to appreciate fully. Memorize this, we say, bury it deep in your consciousness, and mark well where you left it, because someday you'll need it. Sooner or later, you'll need it urgently.

I once heard — or did I dream this? — about a species of bird, a very small bird, that migrates over huge expanses of water. There is great threat in such a journey, but the bird carries a twig in its beak so that when the storms come, it can float on the water, kept from drowning by the twig. And so this psalm has been for many people when the storms come, as they always do on our long journeys.

We know right well, from our own experience, what may have prompted these lines from Samuel Coleridge: "Alone, alone, all, all alone, alone on a wide, wide sea." Yet not alone, replies the psalmist, "for thou art with me."

The verses of this psalm are not only among our earliest memories; they are, for many of us, the last words we hear. I have recited them at countless bedsides, including more than one occasion when a person who had seemingly lost all consciousness moved her lips to silently form the familiar words and taste them one more time: "Even though I walk through the valley of the shadow of death, I fear no evil; for thou art with me."

It is fitting that these are the words that accompany us from the beginning of our lives until the end, because the words themselves speak of God's everlasting presence with us. The everlasting psalm is an audible reminder of the ever-present God.

And then, often these are the words that are spoken at a graveside, to challenge the silence of death. I have an old, tattered Bible that I carry to the graveside, and the page on which this psalm is printed is always easy to find because it has been pebbled and wrinkled from all the rain, the snow, and perhaps also the tears of so many occasions like this. "Thou art with me," we declare, through every stage of our lives, and now, even in this part of life we call death. This God whom we call Light accompanies us even into the darkest valley.

When the psalmist says, "The Lord is my shepherd, I shall not want," clearly he isn't saying that this God fulfills all of our earthly desires. Just as surely it doesn't mean that this God will protect us from all challenge and hardship. The valleys are still dark, evil is still present, the enemies still lurk. This is not a naïvely cheery psalm; it's not full of unremittent sunshine. Pollyanna would choke on some of its words because it talks about life as it really is.

What does the psalmist mean when he begins by saying, "I shall not want"? We want so many things, including those things that the psalmist names: we want death not to claim those we love, we want our enemies to leave us alone, we want evil to be kept at bay. But beneath all of these wants, we want not to be left alone on the wide, wide sea.

So we can see a direct link between the psalmist's declaration "I shall not want" and the affirmation "thou art with me." Beneath all of our wants is the desire for someone who can accompany us through all the shifting and often threatening realities of our lives. We may wish that we could be that presence for one another, but eventually we learn that we cannot.

Every parent knows what it's like to be awakened in the middle of the night by the cries of a child who's had a nightmare. Sometimes the fears are easily quelled: "Daddy, I think there are bears in my closet." "No, there are no bears." "How do you know?" "I'll turn on the light and you'll see."

But other times the fears expressed are not those that are confined to childhood. "Mommy, I'm afraid of being alone." "Daddy, does *everyone* die?" We stumble through our responses. On such occasions we become painfully aware of the limits of words. We're relieved when the child says, "Just stay with me," relieved to learn that the child is seeking not magic words but the gift of presence. We are able to respond easily: "Yes, yes of course I'll stay with you."

Then there is one more question: "Will you stay with me no matter what?" Then it's your turn to sense the stir of fear and to feel tears appear in your own eyes because you know that, although you can stay with the child tonight and, if need be, for many nights in the future, there will come a time, perhaps a night much darker than the child has ever experienced, when she will cry out and you will not be there. This psalm was written for that parent and that child: "I fear no evil, for thou art with me."

Then comes the day that you drop off a child at college. That's when it occurs to you that all you have done as a parent has been in some way a preparation for this day. As you watch her walk with a box of belongings toward the dorm, in many ways she looks like a grown woman, and in other ways like a very small bird.

Later, you're sitting on the bed in the dorm room, all the boxes now in piles. You want to linger. Clearly, she wants you to leave. You want to tell her one more time all the things you want her to remember — words of advice, words of warning, words of encouragement, words of love. You want to wrap her with those words like a continuing embrace and to protect her. But it's all been said before and, besides, it's time to leave. So you put your arms around her and allow yourself just these words: "I love you. You'll be fine." "I know, Dad," she says with a little laugh. "I love you, too." This psalm was also written for such a moment and for such people: "The LORD is my shepherd, I shall not want."

A parishioner in one church I served had just come through a very dark period in her life when she came to see me. For years she had been trapped in a destructive, abusive relationship. There were also some good times along the way, which may explain, in part, why she didn't leave earlier. She never knew which husband would come home at night — the quiet and attentive one, or the one who had been drinking and was surly and sometimes even violent. She never knew what to expect. She explained that she felt like she was always off-balance, like the floor beneath her was always shifting. "And it all happened behind closed doors," she said, "so most people wouldn't have believed me even if I had found the courage to tell them."

This woman knew what it was like to live in the darkest valley. Then, one day, she finally broke for the light and moved out. I asked her, as she looked back, what had sustained her during the darkest times. She replied, "Oh, the support of family, and a lot of prayer, I guess. And — you'll appreciate this because you know I'm not a Bible reader — I also kept thinking about the only verse of Scripture I know, really. I learned it as a child: 'Thou preparest a table before me in the presence of my enemies . . . I fear no evil, for thou art with me.'" Indeed, this psalm was written for such a person, in praise of the One for whom there are no closed doors.

Another time, another place. The nurse comes into the hospital room, with two men behind her filling the doorway. "It's time to go now," she says, sounding more cheerful than seems warranted under the circumstances. The men lift him onto a gurney. "Can I go with him?" "Well, yes, for a ways, if you want." So you walk beside the gurney, trying to hold his hand and look him in the eyes as you go down the wide corridors to the operating room.

The whole homely procession squeezes into the elevator. Everyone is just too quiet, so you say, "I talked with Dr. Harris this morning, and he assures me that the surgeon is the best there is." You've already said this, but your mind is racing and you don't know what else to say. Down another hallway.

It seems very long. It also seems all too short. You reach the doors to the surgical wing. "I have to leave you here, darling. I wish I could go with you." The doors open wide and then close again like the mouth of some great beast.

You stare at the doors, now closed. You try to imagine where he's going and what's happening. Then you go to the waiting room, where some friends have gathered to keep vigil with you. It's good to have them there, good not to have to be alone at such a time. They offer some reassuring words, but the most reassuring words are those of another companion, remembered in silence: "Thou art with me. . . . Surely goodness and mercy shall follow me all the days of my life, and I shall dwell in the house of the LORD forever."

The brief service at the cemetery is over. Everyone stands in silence. There is no breeze on this day, so even the flowers on the coffin are still. The minister has already read from the wrinkled pages of the tattered Bible and offered a prayer. There's nothing left to do. There's nothing left that can be done. All that's left is the rest of your life without the one who is now gone.

No words come to you. It is a moment beyond the reach of words. But before you turn to go to the car, you say one word: "Good-bye." You've said that word so many times, but never like this. And it's just the right word, you know, because it means "God be with you." What else can we say at such a parting that doesn't simply whither and fall at our feet as soon as it is said?

When we say "good-bye," we are expressing a wish — a wish that the psalmist turns into a ringing affirmation: "thou art with me." "God be with you" becomes "God is with me." It is the right wish, and the very right affirmation for such a time, for such a people.

ENDURING LOVE

1 Corinthians 13

THE APOSTLE PAUL'S DESCRIPTION of love in his first letter to the Corinthians is one of the most beloved passages in all of Scripture, and a particular favorite at wedding ceremonies. Even brides and grooms who are relatively unfamiliar with Scripture often request it, sometimes by saying things like, "We'd like to include that love passage. How does it go?" And it is a beautiful hymn to love. Paul, whose writing often can be dense and opaque, here soars to rarefied heights of lyricism: "If I speak in the tongues of mortals and of angels, but do not have love, I am a noisy gong or a clanging cymbal. And if I have prophetic powers, and understand all mysteries and all knowledge, and if I have all faith, so as to remove mountains, but do not have love, I am nothing. . . ." What better words to spin around a couple as they make vows of love? What could be more appropriate than this beautiful tribute to the enduring power of love?

The setting for this passage is quite different, however, from the one in which we usually place it. Paul isn't talking about love in marriage, although what he writes can be applied to such relationships. Rather, he is addressing love in the church. What's more, he's not addressing the Corinthians on a special occasion when everyone is aglow, reveling in the bonds of Christian fellowship — say, just after they've sung a harmonious version of "Blessed Be the Tie that Binds." No, Paul speaks this way about love in a letter addressed to people who are at each other's throats. Instead of picturing people all aglow on a joyful occasion, picture people who are in a white heat of conflict. Paul isn't addressing two people who are choosing to be bound to one another; he's addressing a community of people who have found that the tie binds indeed. It binds and chafes.

Individual members of the Corinthian church were parading their spirituality, comparing themselves to one another and boasting of their superior spiritual gifts, in a classic "mine is better than yours" kind of confrontation. Paul responded by saying that there are many gifts, that people have different gifts, and that each gift is valuable because it can be used to benefit the community of faith. We are like different members of the same body, the body of Christ.

We have different gifts. Some have the gift of wisdom, others the gift of discernment, still others the gift of faith. Of all the spiritual gifts, there is only one that is promised to all. Not everyone is expected to have the gift of wisdom, or discernment, or even faith. There is only one gift of the Spirit that is promised to all, and it is the only gift that is in some way required of all — the gift of love.

Love is a gift of the Spirit that is promised to all because the very nature of God is love. Love is not just an attribute of God, but God's very essence. We are promised the gift of love because God doesn't withhold God's own self from us.

So too all are called to reflect that gift of love. Indeed, the life of a community — whether a community of two in marriage or a community of many in a church — depends upon love for its very existence. A marriage can survive where only one has wisdom or courage, but a marriage cannot long survive where only one has love. Likewise, a church can get along just fine where only some are particularly gifted with faith or the ability to heal. But a church cannot long survive, and certainly cannot fulfill its calling, if only some exhibit the gift of love. So love is the gift that is promised to all, and it is the gift that is required of all.

But how can one speak of "requiring" love? We cannot make ourselves feel a certain way about another person, because we cannot feel on command. And if we happen to feel loving toward someone at one moment, there's no guarantee that we'll feel the same way about the person at another moment.

George S. Kaufman told Irving Berlin that the lyrics of his song "Always" were unrealistic. Instead of "I'll be loving you, always," Kaufman suggested "I'll be loving you, Thursday."

So how can we be required to exhibit the spiritual gift of love when love is fickle and so clearly out of our control, not subject to the command of another or of our own will?

Because the love that Paul commends here is a particular kind of love. It isn't the kind of love we would recognize from the ways in which the word is commonly used in popular songs and greeting cards. This is not romantic love we're talking about here, or even brotherly-sisterly love, but the kind of love God exhibits. The love that Paul commends here is not an emotion, but a form of life that is characterized by self-giving — that is, a Christ-shaped life.

This explains the otherwise strange fact that Paul can go on at length about the gift of love and never once speak of it as an emotion. Instead, he describes love as a way of being and acting. And that way of acting is not soft, sentimental, or in any way mushy. Rather, the love that Paul praises is strong enough and resilient enough that it doesn't need to assert itself, but rather is free to give of itself.

Since such love is a form of life, a cruciform way of life, it is most appropriate to ask not "What does it feel like?" but rather "What does it look like?" That is, it is characterized by actions rather than emotions. And according to Paul, it sure doesn't look like jealousy, or boasting, or arrogance, or rudeness, or resentment. It looks like patience, like kindness, like endurance.

Notice that, in the marriage ceremony, we don't ask the bride and groom "Do you love one another?" Rather, we ask, "*Will* you love one another?" If the love we ask them to affirm were an emotion, we might expect this response: "How do I know if I'm going to love him? This is only Thursday!" But here, as elsewhere, the Gospel seems remarkably uninterested in how we feel and keenly interested in how we act. So when we ask the questions "Will you love this man?" and "Will you love this woman?" we aren't asking the couple to predict how they will feel. Rather, we're asking them to promise to act in a certain way. Will you act in a loving manner, no matter how you feel? Will you put aside boasting and arrogance and rudeness and practice instead acts of patience and kindness — not because you're feeling particularly loving, but perhaps in spite of how you feel in that moment?

My father, drawing on his work as a minister, used to say, "I have concluded that there is one thing necessary for a marriage to succeed. Just one thing." When I was younger, I used to dislike it when he would make sweeping statements like that. One thing? It couldn't be as simple as one thing. And when I wouldn't ask him what that one thing was, he would tell me anyway. "Emotional maturity," he would say. "Both parties need to be emotionally mature. That's the one thing necessary." When I was younger, I always found that answer entirely unsatisfying. What about compatibility? What about an ability to communicate?

But now, many years later — now that I'm about the age my father was when he would make statements like that — I think he was right. For a marriage to succeed, having compatible values helps. The ability to communicate is important. We could extend the list, but checking off everything on the completed list will not assure a successful marriage if the two parties lack emotional maturity. It takes adults, or people willing to become adults, or at least act like adults, for a marriage to succeed. And the same is true of other relationships as well.

And what does "emotional maturity" look like? Well, it sure doesn't look like jealousy, or boasting, or arrogance, or rudeness, or resentment. It looks like patience, like kindness, like endurance. In other words, what my father called emotional maturity looks like Paul's description of love — not an emotion, but a way of acting. It is love with its work clothes on.

In this kind of love, endurance is promised and required as well. Consider a couple celebrating their fortieth wedding anniversary with a quiet dinner for two. The wife picks up her champagne glass, looks her beloved in the eyes, and says, "In spite of everything." Saint Valentine might not approve, but Saint Paul would understand. After all, it was Paul who wrote, "Love bears all things . . . *endures* all things," which is another way of saying that love endures because it puts up with a lot.

That isn't just true in marriage or other relationships between partners — it's true in any relationship. I once had a conversation with someone who was reflecting on the challenge of relating on an ongoing basis with someone who was particularly difficult. "It's an endurance test," she said. "That's what it is — an endurance test." Later I thought, *What a great description.* After all, "to endure" means two different things — to put up with a lot and to last. Two different meanings, and yet, in loving relationships, those two meanings are inextricably related. Love *endures* all things.

That kind of enduring love doesn't come naturally to us.

If I need any verification of that statement, I simply substitute my name for the word "love" in this passage: "Martin is patient and kind; Martin is not jealous or boastful; Martin is not arrogant or rude. Martin does not insist on his own way. . . ." Well, let's just leave it at that, shall we? I think you get the idea. If you want a humbling experience, try using your own name.

And let me show you what I mean when I say that the love Paul describes here is a Christ-shaped love. Try substituting the name of Jesus for love in this passage and listen to how it sounds: "Jesus is patient and kind; Jesus is not jealous or boastful; Jesus is not arrogant or rude. Jesus does not insist on his own way; Jesus is not irritable or resentful; Jesus does not rejoice at wrong, but rejoices in the right. Jesus bears all things, believes all things, endures all things." Now *that* substitution is quite different, isn't it? Different and fitting.

But the love of which Paul speaks, unlike romantic love, or a mother's love for her children, doesn't come naturally to us. It's so clearly beyond us that we can only receive it as a gift from the One who knows how to love in this way, a gift from the One whose very nature is love.

How we pass along that gift in our own lives is bound to be on a very human scale. We will almost certainly express perfect love imperfectly. After all, as Paul puts it, "Now we see in a mirror dimly, but then face to face." That is, there will come a time when we will see one another as Christ sees us, face to face, with the kind of clarity that love permits. There will come a time, Paul affirms, when we will love one another in such a way, and it will come as naturally to us as it did to Christ. In the meantime, there's plenty to do, certainly enough to keep us very busy, as we act out the love that we cannot yet fully claim as our own.

BEING AVAILABLE 24/6

Isaiah 58:13-14

I DON'T RECOMMEND GETTING A FLAT TIRE in the Bronx, at least not during rush hour. I particularly don't recommend getting a flat tire in the Bronx during rush hour after you've already been driving for ten hours. And I most particularly don't recommend getting a flat tire in the Bronx during rush hour, after you've already been driving for ten hours, when you have two young children in the car. (This is a true story. All of my stories are true.) That's what happened to our family a number of years ago when we were driving back home to Vermont after spending a four-month sabbatical at Duke University. Of course I didn't have a jack to change the tire, and this was a time before cell phones. So I had no idea how we would get help. Tall apartment buildings loomed over us like fortresses.

Then a cab pulled over and let out a little woman who was stooped over, as if she were carrying the burdens of New York on her back. I approached her slowly, so as not to seem too threatening, and explained my situation. She invited me in to use her phone.

When I entered her apartment, I was introduced to two other stooped-over women (does living in the Bronx do this to everyone?) and found that the line to the wrecker service was busy. I called every few minutes, and in between I had a chance to learn about the keepers of this oasis of human kindness.

I noticed a sign on the kitchen door saying that it was strictly kosher, and that the kitchen table was set with the Sabbath meal. So as I left to check on my family, I said, "Shabbat shalom" (Sabbath peace), the traditional Jewish Sabbath blessing.

I returned in a few minutes, and we resumed our conversation. They kept saying, "We hope you get through before Shabbat." Then it occurred to me: as observant Jews, they wouldn't use the phone after the sun went down and the Sabbath began.

Now my calls took on a new urgency because I was in a race with the sun. But the sun was making steady progress and I was not. Finally I asked, "You won't use the phone once the Sabbath begins?" My three new friends seemed to be startled by the question. One replied, "No, we will not make any calls, and we won't answer the phone either." It was just as simple, and just as problematic for me, as that. Years later I came across a cartoon in *The New Yorker* that reminded me of this predicament. A Hasidic Jew on the bustling streets of New York is talking on a cell phone, saying, "And remember, if you need anything, I'm available 24/6."

The problem for me was that we were quickly coming upon the seventh day, and I didn't know what to do. Perhaps sensing my reaction, one of the women asked, "Are you a Jewish boy?" Seeing a possible loophole, I perhaps too eagerly responded, "No, no, I'm not Jewish. Not Jewish. No." Then all three laughed and rushed to reassure me by saying over and over, "Oh, *you* can call. We can't, but you go ahead. *You* can call." We all laughed together. With that the sun slowed down and my call finally got through.

As I left their apartment, again exchanging "Shabbat shalom," I felt an incredible sense of gratitude for these women, not only for the ways in which they had helped me, but also for the ways in which they faithfully maintained their religious practices. Nothing in the modern world encouraged them to do so, but the practices made life in that sometimes hostile environment tolerable, just as they have sustained Jews during exile and persecution through the centuries.

The ways these women kept Sabbath can look a lot like confinement, full of restrictions. It can look like a lack of freedom. But we must be careful here, because freedom is often disguised as confinement, and confinement is often disguised as freedom. And this, I think, is just such an instance.

It is telling that the Sabbath was established when the Jews were in exile. Their Babylonian captors wanted to get as much as possible from the Hebrew slaves. So they tried to make them work every day. But the Jews rebelled and insisted that one day a week they would refrain from working so they could worship their God. They said, in essence, "We are good for more than labor. We are made in the image of God. Call us slaves if you must, but one day a week we will remind ourselves that we are precious in the sight of the one true God." Somehow the Babylonians knew that this was a form of rebellion that could not be crushed. And so they relented. One day a week they did not expect the Jews to work and allowed them to worship. So Sabbath, far from being a form of confinement, was a declaration of freedom from the forces that sought to subdue them.

That was a different time and a different place, but I wonder how different it is from our circumstances. In our culture, where getting and spending have been elevated to something like civic duties, to cease working or shopping for a single day is, in itself, a form of rebellion. It is a way of declaring, "We are good for more than labor. We are more than workers and consumers to be judged by the dollars made and the dollars spent." Perhaps we need one day a week to remind ourselves — and to remind the dominant culture — that we were made for more than this. To say "No," even for a day, can begin to sound less like confinement or self-denial and more like freedom.

When my mother was a girl, her family kept the Sabbath quite strictly. In accordance with the biblical mandate, this family of eight children — my mother being the youngest — would observe Sunday as a day of rest. My grandmother would bake bread on Saturday to be served with warm milk the next day — their traditional Sunday supper — so she wouldn't have to cook on the Sabbath. When Sunday arrived, the children wouldn't do their normal chores. The Sunday newspaper was kept on the top shelf of the china cabinet until Monday morning. The children couldn't talk on the telephone, and they weren't allowed to play any games, either.

As a boy, I thought that it sounded awful. My mother would say, "Well, actually, it was my favorite day of the week. After church in the morning, we would spend the day together. It was a busy family, so it was nice to have a day when you could eat dinner together without being so rushed, take walks, and catch up with each other. Or we could spend time with friends."

When I was a boy, listening to my mother's stories, the notion of spending a day a week in such a manner sounded appalling. Now it seems quite appealing, quite wonderful, really — less like a religious obligation and a form of self-denial and more like a gift.

Let's see: You don't have to work. You don't have to cook. You don't have to answer the phone. You just have to praise God and enjoy the day with people you love. As a character in one of the Disney movies put it, "If this is torture, chain me to the wall!" What sounded like confinement when I was a boy now sounds more like freedom.

Just as certainly, what looks at first like freedom may only be confinement in disguise. We have more time-saving devices than ever, and yet we have less time. Those devices all promised us greater freedom. We don't have to wait by the phone anymore; we can take the phone with us. We don't have to walk across town to ask someone a question; we can get an answer effortlessly, almost immediately, through e-mail. I recently saw a billboard, advertising some electronic device, that declared, "Now anyplace can be your workplace." Another billboard proudly announced the beginning of Sunday banking by saying, "Now you can bank when you want to."

That sounds like freedom. But the irony is that all of these devices that claim to offer us greater freedom actually make us feel more and more trapped. You can't get away from the cell phone. That person who e-mailed you expects an instant response. The promise that "Now anyplace can be your workplace" becomes "Now everyplace is your workplace. There is no escape." As for that bank that stays open seven days a week: the wheels of commerce grind on and on relentlessly, and if we get caught up in the grind and don't know how to get out, eventually those wheels grind us up. So we seek refuge in what philosopher William James called "the sin of bustle." We frantically try to keep up with it all, which economist John Kenneth Galbraith compared to the efforts of the squirrel to keep abreast of the wheel that is propelled by his own efforts. So we end up bouncing from this to that, lurching from the pressing to the urgent, bustling from overtime, to overdrive, to overextended, to over and out. Some freedom!

Once I was in a movie theater next to a man who, from the moment he sat down, began working with his BlackBerry hand-held computer and then sending text messages on his cell phone. He continued like that through the entire movie. Occasionally he would look up at the big screen, but then he would bow his head to the tiny screens in his lap. Once there was the buzzing sound of a cell phone set to "ring" silently, and he leapt to his feet and walked to the nearest exit, which happened to be behind the movie screen. There, for a minute or so, you could hear him speaking loudly, as if he were one of the characters on the screen. When he returned to his seat, he watched the movie for a while, but then began to send and receive messages again. I wonder if he ever saw that billboard that announced, "Now anyplace can be your workplace." It sounded like the promise of freedom. But now it looks a lot like confinement.

I was a bit annoyed by this man (this is, after all, another true story), but annoyance wasn't my primary response. My main concern was that his actions had the look and feel of addiction. More and more it seems as if we're addicted to busyness. What I mean is this: It starts with alluring promises: "You'll save time"; "You'll get more done"; "You'll have more freedom." Eventually, however, there's no pleasure in it. We feel trapped. Even though we may begin to sense that our connection to these devices isn't good for us, we no longer see a way out. We're stuck in patterns we didn't exactly choose, but we don't know how to change them. What began as a promise of freedom ends up being a confinement from which we see no escape.

Janis Joplin famously sang, "Freedom's just another word for nothing left to lose." Well, those of us who are addicted to busyness seem to have done Janis Joplin one better: "Freedom's just another word for nothing more to give."

A few years ago there was a wonderful group of folks in our congregation who wanted to celebrate Christmas differently. They thought that the season had lost some of its luster. The focus had somehow become misplaced. There was too much commercialization, too much money spent on things that no one really needed and only vaguely wanted. And, perhaps most of all, there was too much rushing from Christmas this to Christmas that, too much bustle, too much stress. I was very much in sympathy with their aims and encouraged their efforts. It had the feel of a movement. Only one obstacle stood in their way: the group couldn't find a time to meet because their schedules were too packed. There was no time when they could get together to talk about how we might have more time during the holidays. That experience seems something like a parable of our age.

A friend of mine, speaking of the time she was a pastor, told me she always felt that she had to make herself available at any hour, no matter where she was, every day of the year. Looking back, she observed, with no small sense of irony, "There used to be a time when only God was that important."

It is precisely that reminder, that "only God is that important," that is the basis of the practice of keeping Sabbath. When we stop working for a time, we can see that the world can manage very well without us. The sun still rises and sets. The tides still ebb and flow. We are fed. We are not indispensable, but we are valued nonetheless. It's good to have that reminder on occasion. In fact, it's essential.

The practice of Sabbath, however, is not essentially a stern reminder, nor is it primarily a set of rules about what you can and cannot do. It's meant to be received as a gift. Worshiping with Jews on Friday night, I am always so struck by the deep sense of gratitude for the gift of Sabbath that is so much a part of Jewish tradition. Barbara Brown Taylor, a Christian reflecting on the place of Sabbath in Israel, writes, "On that one day every week, they remembered their worth lay not in their own productivity but in God's primordial love for them. Sabbath offered them a foretaste of heaven, when they would lie back in God's arms and behold the glory of creation for all eternity."[1]

Far from an onerous duty, the Sabbath is a day, in the

---

1. Barbara Brown Taylor, "Remember the Sabbath," *Christian Century,* May 5, 1999.

words of Isaiah, "to take delight in the LORD." It is a day to enjoy God's creation by pausing, and resting, and eating, and tasting, and smelling, and listening, and noticing, and talking, and not talking, and breathing, and sleeping, and touching. The Talmud prescribes the Sabbath as a time for making love. It is a time for those things that bring delight and remind us of God's goodness and constant care for us.

So the Sabbath is a gift, but through the centuries, the people of God have been so reluctant to accept it that God had to make it a command: "Remember the Sabbath day and keep it holy." It is as if God were saying, "Take the gift. I insist. You'll end up thanking me."

MEMORY AND PERSONHOOD

Psalm 139:1-12

I REMEMBER THE FIRST TIME my grandmother wasn't able to recognize me, the first time it was clear that she didn't remember who I was. I was in high school at the time. The look on her face revealed that she had no idea who had just walked into her room. "It's me, Grandmother. It's Martin." The expression on her face — if one could call it that — did not change. She was the only grandparent I ever knew, and because my father was an only child, she had only three grandchildren — not many to keep track of, but there is no memory, however precious, that is immune to the ravages of severe dementia.

My grandmother and I were not particularly close. To be frank, even when she was well, my siblings and I always experienced her as a rather formal and distant woman. Her dementia only added to that sense of distance, because there is nothing quite so distancing as a loss of memory. As her memory receded, the focus of her world narrowed, until she was only able to recognize my father, her only child, the one upon whom, in other stages of her life, the sun rose and the sun set. And then, her memory reached the vanishing point, when she could no longer remember even my father.

When my father died quite suddenly, we went to tell my grandmother the news — news she was not able to comprehend. But we thought we should say something. In a way, we were grateful that she couldn't take in this news, because it would have been overwhelming. In a sense, dementia saved her from grief, so there was some comfort in that. Still, her only child had died, and it seemed unspeakably sad that she couldn't remember him, or recognize his name, or mark the loss.

When my grandmother herself died a number of years later, we said things like, "She wasn't herself for many years. This wasn't Grandmother. She left us a long time ago." I have since heard similar thoughts expressed many times, when someone has died after a long illness, and particularly after a long and losing struggle with dementia. "She left us a long time ago."

One could make the case that, to a significant degree, we are what we remember. Ralph Waldo Emerson, in an essay entitled simply "Memory," writes,

> [Memory] is the thread on which the beads of man are strung, making the personal identity which is necessary for moral action. Without it, all life and thought were an unrelated succession. As gravity holds matter from flying off into space, so memory gives stability to knowledge; it is the cohesion which keeps things from falling into a lump, or flowing in waves.[1]

Elsewhere Emerson writes of memory as the personification of a divine presence:

> Memory performs the impossible for man by the strength of his divine arms; holds together past and present, beholding

---

1. Ralph Waldo Emerson, "Memory," in *Memory: An Anthology*, ed. Harriet Harvey Wood and A. S. Byatt (London: Vintage Books, 2009), pp. 172-73.

both, existing in both, abides in the flowing, and gives continuity and dignity to human life. It holds us to our family, to our friends.[2]

Our memories are so much a part of who we are that it can be hard to imagine who we would be without them. What if I no longer remembered what it was like to grow up in my family? What if I could no longer remember my parents and what it was like to feel so completely loved by them, which I have always thought of as the origin and source of my sense of self-esteem? Or what if I no longer remembered the times of bonding with friends? Or what it was like to feel the stir of a call to ministry? Or to fall in love with my wife, Karen? Or what if I forgot about the birth of our children — or that I even have children? Or forgot the face of my wife? Or what prayer is? If I could no longer remember what it is to be Martin Copenhaver, would I still be Martin Copenhaver? In what sense would I be a different person — or a person at all — if I no longer remembered? If I lost much or all of my memory, might someone say about me, "He left us a long time ago"? So, yes, one could make the case that, to a significant degree, we are what we remember.

But, just as surely, we are more than our memories. We don't say of an infant, living in those early months before memory, "Well, she's not yet arrived. She's not yet a person." When we baptize her, we don't say, "It's too bad that she isn't yet a person, someone who can remember events like this." We affirm that such an infant is indeed a person, even without memory — not yet all that she is to be and yet, from the beginning, a full and growing person. The truth is that we're

2. Ralph Waldo Emerson, *Natural History of the Intellect* (Chicago: Wrightwood Press, 2008), p. 33.

always changing, always gaining and relinquishing, grabbing hold and letting go — of relationships, of abilities, of memories, at every stage of our lives.

A loss of memory doesn't make us any less a person. In fact, I've learned that equating personhood and rationality is a peculiarly Western notion. The Eastern Orthodox tradition puts less emphasis on rationality as the criterion for human status, and more emphasis on the person in relationship. According to that tradition, we are who we are not so much because of what we remember; rather, we are who we are through how we're remembered by others in community.

What if we acted out the understanding that those who no longer can remember the prayers of the church, or the Bible stories, or the hymns, have a special place in the church because it is a community that remembers the prayers and stories for those people, and sings the hymns on their behalf when they no longer can? What if we are the ones who remember for them? And what would it require to be that kind of community?

In the end, what ensures our personhood is that we are remembered by God. It is true that throughout Scripture we are reminded to remember, told to remember, commanded to remember — that, in some sense, remembering is an act of faith: "Forget not all God's benefits." In the end, however, here as elsewhere, what matters ultimately is not our actions, but God's actions. If we do not remember God or God's benefits, God still remembers us.

Isaiah asks, "Can a woman forget her nursing child, or show no compassion for the child of her womb?" And the answer is, "Yes. Tragically. Sometimes, yes." But Isaiah quickly adds these words, which he takes to be God's very assurance: "Even these may forget, yet I will not forget you. See, I have inscribed you on the palms of my hands." It is as if God says, "You are not something I merely hold in my hands, because something that is held can be dropped. You are not something that is merely written on my hands, because what is merely written can be washed off or worn away. No, you are *inscribed* on the palms of my hands. You are marked on the palms of my hands in a way that cannot disappear or even fade. I will not forget you. Even if you forget me, I will not forget you. I hold you dear and always will."

Psalm 139 reminds us that God will not let us go, or let us go alone. God accompanies us, through triumph and trial, through the heights and the depths:

> *Where can I go from your spirit?*
> *Or where can I flee from your presence?*
> *If I ascend to heaven, you are there;*
> *If I make my bed in Sheol — in the shadowy pit — you are*
>   *there.*

We might add:

> *If I ascend to the heights of rationality, you are there;*
> *If my memory leaves me altogether, you are there.*

As I noted earlier, it is true that throughout Scripture we are reminded to remember, told to remember, commanded to remember. But, thank God, Scripture always points beyond our actions to God's actions. And God will always remember us.

The psalmist continues:

> *You knit me together in my mother's womb.* . . .
> *My frame was not hidden from you,*
> *When I was being made in secret,*
> *Intricately woven in the depths of the earth.*

We might add:

And even now, at the other end of my life,
In a different kind of darkness than the darkness of my
    mother's womb,
The darkness of forgetfulness,
Even there I am not hidden from you.
Once again, as always, you see me, and know me.

We are so much more than what we remember. We are what God remembers.

OUR CLOSE AND
DISTANT GOD

Exodus 33:7-23

S OMEONE ONCE OBSERVED THAT if you take the paradox out of religion, you get a preacher. Well, I am a preacher, but I'm determined to prove that person wrong. I want to take up one of the paradoxes of the Christian faith. If that paradox doesn't remain when I'm finished, or even if I unwittingly diminish the tension of that paradox somewhere along the way, I will have failed. You see, this paradox isn't on some fringe that can be trimmed from the Christian understanding of our relationship with God; rather, it stands indispensably at the center.

Picture a church study group whose participants are sharing their experiences of the presence of God in their lives. Someone says, "The other day I was praying, just telling God about what's going on with me these days, particularly about my son, who can't seem to find his direction in life, and I know this may sound crazy — particularly because I'm not sure I can explain it in a way that makes sense to me — but it was as if I heard God whisper, 'It's going to be all right.' It wasn't a voice exactly. But it was as clear as a voice — and very comforting."

Another member of the group responds with a little laugh. "I'm so glad you said that, because if you're crazy, then so am I.

I had a similar experience when I came in early for worship a few weeks ago. I was sitting in the pew by myself, thinking about my husband, who died last year, feeling empty and just kind of dead myself. And, like you, I wonder how this sounds, but in that moment I sensed someone's presence. It was so real that I almost turned around to see who it was, even though I knew that no one was behind me. Anyway, I knew even then and I'm convinced now that it was God's way of saying, 'I am closer than you imagine. Lean on me.'"

Have you ever had times like that, times when God seemed unspeakably close? Or is your experience quite different?

William Beebe was a naturalist who would visit Theodore Roosevelt at his home in Sagamore Hill. After an evening's talk, the two men would go out on the lawn and gaze up at the sky and see who could detect the faint spot of light-mist beyond the Square of Pegasus. Then one or the other would ritually recite, "That is the Spiral Galaxy in Andromeda. It is as large as our Milky Way. It is one of a hundred million galaxies. It is 750,000 light years away. It consists of a hundred billion suns, each larger than our sun." After an interval, Roosevelt would grin at Beebe and say, "Now I think we're small enough. Let's go to bed."[1]

I often think of this story as I'm walking along the long, sandy beaches of Fire Island, where my family has gone every summer for many years. The enormity of the ocean itself has a way of putting me in my place, but then I remember what I once heard an astronomer say: there are more stars in the universe than there are grains of sand in the world. I don't know how he calculated that, but it's a remarkable comparison. Reach down and pick up a handful of sand, and you're holding a galaxy. Countless solar systems come up between

---

1. Quoted in Paul Lee Tan, *Encyclopedia of 7,700 Illustrations* (Cleveland, Tenn.: Assurance Publishers, 1990).

your toes with every step. And as far as you can see in either direction there is sand. It is, quite literally, awe-inspiring.

Have you ever had an experience like that, a time when you've felt overwhelmed by the enormity — or the intricacy — of the universe? And has that ever created within you an overpowering sense of awe at the majesty of the God who set the stars in their courses and rules over them still? It's not always a welcome sensation.

In one of H. G. Wells's novels there is the story of a man of stature whose mind was so tense and strained that he was in serious danger of a complete nervous breakdown. His doctor told him that the only thing that could save him was to find the peace that fellowship with God can give. "What!" the man exclaimed. "To think of that, up there, having fellowship with me! I would as soon think of cooling my throat with the Milky Way or shaking hands with the stars!"[2] Has God ever seemed that mighty and that distant to you?

So, which is it? Is God unspeakably close or unimaginably distant? Is God the intimate friend with whom we can share our lives, or is God the distant ruler who is too mighty to grasp or, at times, even approach? Usually when people speak of God they speak in one way or the other. But the paradox is that God is always both. In the words of a communion liturgy, God is "as close to us as breathing and distant as the farthest star." The same God who seems to whisper in our ear also makes the waterfalls roar. The same God who can shake the very foundations of the earth also comes to us like a reassuring tap on the shoulder.

Scripture maintains the integrity of the paradox. Moses pitches a tent he calls "the tent of meeting," and there Moses and the Lord chat together. It is an intimate time because,

---

2. H. G. Wells, quoted in William Barclay, *The Lord's Prayer* (Louisville: Westminster John Knox Press, 1998), p. 31.

as the author of Genesis puts it, "the LORD used to speak to Moses . . . as one speaks to a friend." A fragment of one of those conversations follows. The Lord has already promised to usher the people of Israel into the Promised Land, and further promised that they will forever be God's people. Moses asks for more. He says, "Show me your ways, so that I may know you and find favor in your sight."

God replies, "My presence will go with you, and I will give you rest."

Moses shoots back, "If your presence will not go, do not carry us up from here," which might be translated, "Hey, you'd better go with us because this isn't the kind of journey we would make on our own." And the Lord, like a parent who succumbs to the entreaties of a child, says, "I will do the very thing you have asked."

By any measure it is a remarkable conversation, the kind of open, easy exchange one might expect between two people who know each other very well. But then Moses goes one step further. He asks, "Show me your glory, I pray." That is, show me the essence of your being. Let me see you.

The Lord responds by saying, "You cannot see my face, for no one shall see me and live." Then the Lord instructs Moses to go to the cleft of a rock. The Lord tells Moses that before the divine glory passes by, the Lord will cover the cleft with the divine hand. Then, when the Lord has passed, the hand will be lifted for a moment to let Moses see not the Lord's face, but the Lord's back. Just a peek, mind you, a glimpse and nothing more, for anything more would destroy Moses as surely as the sun melts ice.

See the paradox: The Lord spoke to Moses as one speaks to a friend. And yet, Moses was given only a sliver of a glance at God's back. To Moses the Lord remained both unspeakably close and unimaginably distant.

It is difficult to maintain the paradox, but see how important it is: if we use only the language of intimacy to describe our relationship with God, then God is reduced to the status of a familiar buddy whose ways are easily grasped. There is a presumptuous chumminess about it, like that of the actress Jane Russell, who once declared, "God is just a livin' doll!" As the theologian Karl Barth once insisted, using the language of another time, "'God' is not 'Man' said with a loud voice." God is greater than we can grasp with our experience, beyond the limits of our imaginations. There are times when we can speak of God with ease and intimacy, but then we need to be reminded that there is such power in God's name that if we utter it we need to stand back as surely as if we have unleashed a flash of lightning.

If we speak only of God's majesty and power, however, something else is missing. Such unalloyed awe soon hardens into unrelenting fear. We feel swept away like a particle of sand, disappearing into the vastness of creation. God becomes like the monarch who is too busy with the affairs of the world to do more than wave from the window of a distant tower. Surely we long for more than this. As the well-known preacher Harry Emerson Fosdick once put it, "A God who doesn't care doesn't count."

Nevertheless, Moses' experience of God embraced both: somehow God was simultaneously as close as breathing and as distant as the farthest star. Although both the intimacy and the majesty of God can be overwhelming to us, we learn from Moses that we don't have to take in that reality all at once, at least not face to face.

I think that is what C. S. Lewis was getting at when he thanked a friend for what that friend taught him about prayer. Lewis wrote,

> You first taught me the great principle, "Begin where you are."
> I had thought one had to start by summoning up what we

believe about the goodness and greatness of God, by thinking about creation and redemption and "all the blessings of this life." You turned to the brook and once more splashed your burning face and hands in the little waterfall and said, "Why not begin with this."[3]

Begin with this — with the water cupped in your hands, a glimpse of God's back. It can be enough . . . for a time.

But then we confront Jesus. In him the paradox of the closeness and the power of God is not diminished but is presented most starkly. In Jesus the distant and majestic creator of the heavens and the earth became Emmanuel, that is, "God with us." He is as close to us as our own lives, as familiar as the way home, and yet also, at the same time, the fullest expression of God's power and glory.

God said to Moses, "Go and stand in the cleft of the rock, and I will cover it with my hand, and then when I have passed I will lift my hand, and you will catch a glimpse of my back, for if you look into my face you will surely die."

But then, in the person of Jesus, it is as if God said, "I will come to you in the person of a simple carpenter, born in a small corner of a big world, that all might have eternal life. In him the fullness of God is pleased to dwell. He will be as close as your own elbow and yet encompass the dimensions of eternity. And through this One you shall see me and not die. You will live to tell the story and live as you have never lived before."

Which is to say, in Jesus, God turned around, and finally we could see that face.

3. C. S. Lewis, *Letters to Malcolm: Chiefly on Prayer* (Boston: Houghton Mifflin Harcourt, 2002), p. 88.

TO SAVE OR TO SAVOR?

Mark 14:3-9

NO WONDER JESUS' DISCIPLES are confused. After all, the call to help those in need looms large in Jesus' life and words. Jesus had told them in the clearest terms that it will be those who have fed the hungry, clothed the naked, and sheltered the homeless who will be received by the Lord with benedictions, and those who have failed to do so who will be sent empty away. The disciples also remembered the way Jesus responded to the rich young ruler when he asked about how he might inherit eternal life. "Go, sell all you have; give it to the poor," Jesus replied. "Then, come, and we'll talk about eternal life." That seemed clear enough.

But now the disciples are eating a simple supper with Jesus when in bursts a woman carrying an alabaster jar filled with precious ointment — the kind of ointment that was usually reserved for the anointing of a king or the burial of a wealthy person. This woman — either because she's nervous or because she wants to make clear that she's not leaving that room until the ointment is all used — breaks the alabaster jar and pours the ointment over Jesus' head. It strikes the disciples as an unconscionable extravagance. But what makes the whole episode so difficult to take in is that Jesus does nothing to stop her and says nothing. He simply receives the gift.

The disciples seethe and mutter with righteous indignation, "Why was the ointment wasted in this way? It must have cost almost a year's wages. It could have been sold and the money given to the poor."

So the disciples, perhaps thinking that Jesus is using the occasion to give them a kind of test, reproach the woman. Surely that's the correct response. But Jesus intervenes, saying, "Leave her alone; why do you trouble her? She has done a beautiful thing to me. For you always have the poor with you, and whenever you will, you can do good to them, but you will not always have me."

"Well, make up your mind," the disciples must have been tempted to say. No wonder they were confused.

And there are times when Jesus' disciples still seem confused. The largest Gothic structure in the world is St. John the Divine Episcopal Cathedral in Manhattan. According to the original designs, made at the beginning of the twentieth century, the cathedral was to have two ornate and graceful spires. But then the money ran out. And before sufficient funds could be raised to complete the construction, the neighborhood changed. St. John the Divine became a Gothic island in a sea of poverty. The plans to build the spires were shelved. The cathedral devoted its resources to serving the poor of the neighborhood. In the 1960s there was even talk of selling the cathedral, using a small portion of the proceeds to build a more modest structure, and dedicating the balance to the cathedral's outreach ministries. Then, twenty years later, the bishop declared that now more than ever the neighborhood needed a symbol of the majesty and glory of God. The old plans were dusted off, and those in charge began to build the spires, importing the finest Italian stone masons to do the job, which eventually cost millions. In one historical moment they were talking about selling the property and giving the proceeds to the poor; in the next they were pouring millions into an architectural extravagance. Are Jesus' disciples still confused?

This same tension also hits close to home and in countless ways. How can I squander almost four bucks on a cone of Häagen-Dazs ice cream when little children are starving in Africa? How can a church justify spending hundreds of thousands of dollars on a pipe organ when there are villages in Latin America with no sewers? How can a city support a symphony orchestra while public schools have their funding cut? It seems that we too are confused. What are we to do? What does God expect?

E. B. White framed the issue with characteristic clarity: "If the world were merely seductive, that would be easy. If it were merely challenging, that would be no problem. But I arise in the morning torn between a desire to improve the world, and a desire to enjoy the world. That makes it hard to plan the day."[1]

In planning our days, confused as we are about how we are to spend them, we sometimes try the via media, the middle way. Perhaps we need to do things in moderation. Perhaps if the woman who approached Jesus had had a measuring cup, she could have used half the ointment to anoint Jesus and sold the other half and given the money to the poor. Did St. John the Divine really need two spires? Wouldn't one have been adequate? Or if they insisted on two spires, did they have to be so tall? Wouldn't short spires give sufficient glory to God?

Or, if we're having ice cream, does it have to be Häagen-Dazs? Couldn't it be non-fat frozen yogurt instead? And does a city really need a whole orchestra? Wouldn't a string quartet do? Or perhaps finding the middle way means that when

---

1. E. B. White, quoted in *The Collected Sermons of William Sloane Coffin* (Louisville: Westminster John Knox Press), p. 296.

we serve the poor or sit in the concert hall, we shouldn't get too carried away with either one. Serve the poor, but don't let yourself get too involved. Enjoy the concert, but not too much. Is that the middle way? Haven't we always heard that all things should be done in moderation?

But then this woman bursts in on the dinner and pours the whole jar of ointment on Jesus' head. She gave of herself, as Jesus said in another context, "in good measure, pressed down, shaken together, running over" (Luke 6:38). She didn't pour out a few drops and say, "Well, I guess that ought to be enough for this occasion." Her expression of devotion wasn't smothered by caution or prudence. She didn't count the cost. She was lifted clear out of arithmetic and into love — one of the greatest leaps a life can take. It was in response to that kind of extravagant gesture that Jesus said, "She has done a beautiful thing." It seems that Jesus thinks we are meant to get carried away.

In fact, at no point does Jesus praise or practice moderation. Jesus reserved his praise for the likes of the woman in the temple who gave two copper coins, everything she had — no moderation in that. When the rich young ruler approached him, he told the man to sell all that he had and give the money to the poor — no moderation there, either. When the wine ran out at a wedding feast, Jesus turned six jars of water into wine. That was equivalent to 180 gallons, more than enough for any party — an extravagant gesture. There is no such thing as moderate extravagance. And Jesus is all for extravagance: extravagant devotion, extravagant celebration, extravagant forgiveness, extravagant service, extravagant giving, and extravagant receiving — because only extravagance is an appropriate response to the God who pours gifts upon us all, and always with extravagance.

But if this is so, how do we plan the day? We can't do all things with extravagance at the same time.

Malcolm Muggeridge tells a wonderful story about Mother Teresa of Calcutta in his book *Something Beautiful for God*. Muggeridge was a brilliant, hard-bitten journalist, a confirmed curmudgeon, who went to Calcutta to do a story about Mother Teresa, having heard about her remarkable ministries to the destitute and dying of that city. While he was there, Muggeridge became keenly aware that Mother Teresa's order, the Missionaries of Charity, were always running out of money. And when they did, Mother Teresa would tell the sisters, "Then you must beg. Begging, when it is for Christ, is a very beautiful activity." Muggeridge writes, "Despite this chronic financial stringency of the Missionaries of Charity, when I was instrumental in steering a few hundred pounds in Mother Teresa's direction, she astonished, and I must say enchanted, me by expending it on the chalice and paten for her new novitiate, 'so,' she wrote, 'you will be daily on the altar close to the Body of Christ.'"[2]

Hearing that story, we might well wonder: Didn't that woman know any better? She could have used the money to serve the poor. But instead she blew it all on a chalice and paten for some young novitiate and a jaded old journalist. And now, because of this foolish extravagance, she'd be back on the street the next day, begging.

This story reminds me that the Christian life is not about moderation or even about consistency. It is, instead, about rhythm, and our task is to reflect the extravagant dimensions of this great rhythm that pulses through all of life like a heartbeat. There is a time to be born and a time to die; a time to plant and a time to pluck up what is planted; a time to mourn and a time to dance; a time to keep and a time to cast away; a time to save the world and a time to savor the world.

2. Malcolm Muggeridge, *Something Beautiful for God* (San Francisco: Harper & Row, 1971), p. 130.

To be sure, one can get stuck on one side of this dynamic rhythm, which can be about as dangerous as only inhaling or only exhaling.

Perhaps the dangers of only savoring the world are so clear and so close that we need not dwell on them. Such lives are characterized by self-indulgence and extravagant self-concern. And, no doubt, that is the direction toward which most of our own lives naturally incline. Our entire culture tilts in this direction, and there are evident dangers in doing so.

But just as certainly there are dangers in only serving the world. To only serve the world and never to savor it is to be only the giver of gifts and never the receiver. It may be more blessed to give than to receive, but sometimes giving is a whole lot easier. Constant giving puts us in a superior position. It means, among other things, that we never have to say thank you, and there is a certain arrogance in that. We are called to graciously receive a gift that is graciously given. This is particularly true of the extravagant gifts of everyday life: listening to the final movement of Beethoven's Ninth Symphony; spending a spring morning picking a palette of wildflowers; sitting on the porch with a glass of iced tea with a fresh sprig of mint, letting the late afternoon unfold at the leisurely pace of a novel; turning up the volume when one of your favorite songs comes on the radio so that you can dance in your kitchen; even enjoying a cone of Häagen-Dazs (chocolate fudge with chocolate chips, double scoop). Any of those things can be a celebration of the God from whom all good gifts come.

One's life depends on doing both, serving and savoring, giving and receiving — not at the same time, of course, because that may not be possible, but each in turn at the appropriate time. Which is another way of saying that one's life depends on being inconsistent in the way that all who both breathe in and breathe out are inconsistent.

So the life Jesus commends is not so much about consistency or moderation, or even balance. Rather, it is about allowing the grand, extravagant sweeps of this dynamic to be reflected in our lives. Mother Teresa begged for pennies to serve the poor. But when she received a sizable sum as a gift, she lavished it upon a seeming extravagance, and then, because the poor are always with us, she was back on the street the next day, begging again. If that is inconsistent, it is the kind of inconsistency that reflects this great dynamic of the Christian life, giving and receiving and giving again, as inconsistent as only the two steps of a dance might be. Receiving and giving, inhaling and exhaling.

It is telling that St. John the Divine Cathedral didn't cut back their ministries to the poor when they began the construction of those magnificent spires. Rather, somehow their ministries to the poor have been able to increase — reflecting God's extravagance in both directions. A deep inhale, a deep exhale, an extravagant gesture in one direction and then in the other.

This approach to life isn't easy or consistent. I think we're supposed to struggle with these matters — and our Scripture doesn't let us off the hook. Only you know toward which direction your own life leans, and which part of the message you need most to hear. After all, it was the woman whose life had been mostly duty whom Jesus encouraged in her moment of extravagance. But it was to the rich young ruler, whose life had been mostly extravagance, to whom Jesus said, "Go, sell what you have, and give it to the poor."

Wherever we might find ourselves, I think we're meant to struggle within the life-giving swings of this dynamic approach to life. This also means that, as someone once said in another context, if you're not confused, at least occasionally, then you don't understand the situation.

Our lives as Christians were not meant to be easy to plan,

or easy to carry out. Instead, they were meant to reflect the extravagance of God in giving and in receiving, in saving and in savoring, as we enjoy the world and attempt to improve it. We need to remember that we were created to sway to the rhythmic patterns of God's grace.

JOB'S FRIENDS

Job 2:11-13; 5:17-18; 8:2-6; 11:13-17; 13:4b-5

THROUGH THE THOUSANDS OF YEARS that Job's story has been told, his friends have been much criticized. Their words have been characterized as insensitive and uncaring. If, however, we remember times when we have tried to console the sorrowing, I think our judgment of them will be less harsh. Then we will remember how our own attempts at consolation have felt so clumsy, our words so woefully inadequate. Novelist James Worley could have been speaking of Job's friends, or of us when we have tried to be a friend, when he wrote, "The best one can do in sympathy is fumble at the edges of another's misery with callused fingertips and an awkward heart."

Job's friends were responding to misfortune on an epic scale. One day Job was the richest man around, and the next day he was wiped out. His oxen and camels were stolen. When lightning struck his sheep barn, the entire flock, not to mention the hired hands, went up in smoke. His seven sons and three daughters were having a rousing party when a hurricane came along and made the house a crumbled tomb for all who were inside. Then Job came down with leprosy. So Job cursed the day he was born — who can blame him? — and prayed for the release of death.

And yet, even then his own heart mocked him by continuing to beat.

When Job's friends heard about all of this, they did what good friends do — they decided to pay a call. Perhaps on the way over to Job's house they rehearsed in their minds what they would say to him. After all, it's so difficult to know what to say. When they first saw Job, they didn't even recognize him. And when they did recognize him — like a living ghost — they were struck dumb. It was Jewish custom that taught them to show their grief by tearing their robes, but their tears came unbidden, rich and natural, as if from a spring in the center of their being. For seven days and seven nights they sat with Job and said nothing, sharing the silence as friends might share a meal.

Then, on the eighth day, it was Job himself who first broke the silence. He opened his heart, and torrents of despair rushed out. When he finished, the seal of silence now broken, each of the friends in turn offered words of consolation. It's hard to determine whether they spoke primarily because they felt Job needed to hear what they had to say, or because they needed to hear it themselves, but I'm sure it was a little of both. We all experience the need to order life with words, to make sense of tragedy, even when it's not our own. We want to know that there's a reason behind what happens. Every unexplained tragedy is a threat to our very selves — a threat we may attempt to ward off with our words of consolation.

At the very least, we can say that if Job's needs were foremost in their minds, they wouldn't have chosen the words they did. The balm they applied to Job's wounds was mostly salt.

One friend seemed to say that suffering is a kind of purification for the soul. He advised Job to use his suffering as an opportunity for self-improvement.

A second friend expressed the conviction that Job's suffering must be a form of punishment. He advised Job to repent. If he did, God would reward him with a life that was even better than the one he had before.

A third friend said that Job's trials must be a kind of test of his faith. He told Job that we are not meant to understand what is behind God's actions, but that's part of the test too — to see if we can worship God even without any understanding.

Although the three friends each tried different ways to comfort Job and explain his trials, all three struck similar themes: God punishes the evil and rewards the good. God's mercy is directed toward those who fear God. If catastrophe has overtaken someone, it must be that the person has sinned. Let him or her repent, and deliverance is sure.

The familiar expression "the patience of Job" comes from the New Testament book of James. But in Job's own book, he's not exactly patient. Job is more than a little impatient with his friends. When they had finished their attempts at comfort, he said, "I wish you'd shut your mouths — silence is your only claim to wisdom."

In these very words Job points to the first thing we can learn about how to befriend the suffering: we should not be too quick to fill the silence. Sometimes the wisest thing is to respect the silence of the sorrowing, and to share it with them. Silence is part of the language of grief, and we must learn that language if we are to share the sorrow of the grieving. When Job's friends first came to him, they sat in silence for seven days and nights, silence that was punctuated with tears. And though the silence may have been awkward for the friends, I imagine it was nourishing for Job. Then, finally, Job brought his wounds to speech, as the grieving will eventually find the need to do. It is then that Job's friends felt the need to respond, which was perhaps their first mistake. "If only you'd shut your mouths," said Job. "Silence is your only claim to wisdom."

When we see a friend who has experienced tragedy, we probably wouldn't say just what Job's friends said. But I do think we sometimes make similar mistakes with our words.

Sometimes we also make the mistake of assuming that our role is to make suffering explainable. We offer reasons why this must have happened. We go with a theory to meet a person — which, in itself, should tell us that our efforts are doomed from the start. In response to tragedy, I don't often hear people say, as Job's friends did, "God must be punishing him." More often the words spoken are gentler, even if they're headed in the same direction — words such as "Perhaps this was given to you as an opportunity to grow." Or, "This must be part of some larger plan." One response I commonly hear in the face of death is "God must have wanted her with him."

We say one thing, and then another, trying everything we can think of without really thinking through the implications of what we're saying. We try one thing and then another, like a doctor who knows of no cure and so, in desperation, tries whatever medicine is close at hand. But, try as we might, such attempts at explanation are never sufficient. They're too shallow to reach the depths of our need. No one in history has been able to explain suffering, and many have tried. It is an intractable mystery that has eluded the keenest minds and humbled the most faithful souls. To offer explanations is to say more than we know.

Notice also that such explanations are usually offered at the expense of God. God is depicted as a cruel snatcher of souls or as a vengeful punisher of the weak, which often makes the person who has suffered want to have nothing more to do with the very One who can be of most help — God.

And, like Job's friends, we can sometimes make the mistake of assuming that our role is to give advice to those who suffer. We may not give the advice, as Job's friends did, that the sorrowing should repent. But those who have undergone trials usually receive advice from every quarter: Do this. Try that. Get on with your life. Focus on the positive. Get out more.

The twenty-one-year-old son of a man I knew was murdered, innocently caught in a crossfire of bullets, just as many who suffer tragedy are merely caught in the crossfire of life. When the father received word of his son's death, he happened to be at a weekend conference conducted by a nationally famous minister. When he approached the minister to tell him why he had to rush home, the minister immediately gave him this advice: "In your grief, just be thankful for the twenty-one good and long years you enjoyed with your son." I don't find it hard to understand why this advice didn't satisfy the father, because it doesn't satisfy me. Advice in the midst of tragedy seldom does. It lasts about as long as a handkerchief in a blast furnace.

If explanations of tragedy usually belittle God, advice offered in the face of tragedy can belittle the pain of the grieving. Advice can end up implying that a person's pain is something small, when in fact the person who is bearing that pain is more likely to experience it as something overwhelmingly large. Rather than expressing a kind of reverence before loss and sorrow, advice belittles it. After all, if one's pain is so easily managed, if all one needs to do is follow this advice, then that pain cannot be of any great scope or depth. It's difficult to face hardship on a large scale, but it's even more difficult if those around the one who grieves attempt to diminish it with advice.

Job's friends can teach us a lesson in how not to "comfort" those who have experienced sorrow or tragedy. We should not be too quick to fill the silence of sorrow. Explanations are not called for. Advice is not what is needed. Rather, we must offer something else.

But what might that something be? Theologian Paul

Scherer put it well: "The soul in its deep distress seeks not light but warmth, not counsel but understanding." Which is to say, I think Job's friends had it right at first. They came to Job and — for seven days at least — they found the courage and faith to share his sorrow, even though they didn't have explanations or answers. *Courage* and *faith* are just the words I want to use here, for it takes a measure of these virtues to share unexplained tragedy with a friend.

Those seven days that Job's friends sat with him reflect the Jewish custom of sitting shiva. In Jewish tradition, a grieving family stays home for seven days and receives visitors, but according to this tradition, visitors sit in silence with the family — unless or until a member of the family addresses them. Only then is a visitor permitted to speak. I think the tradition of sitting shiva is so specific on this point because it is difficult not to fill the silence.

When we are with someone who has experienced loss or hardship, we need to trust that our gifts of friendship are sufficient. Before tragedy strikes, our love seems sufficient, our expressions of care seem enough. But when tragedy strikes, we often feel as if something else, something new, something more is required. We feel as if we must now have explanations and answer questions, explanations that were never required of us before, answers that, under normal circumstances, friends aren't expected to supply. We seek something new to say or do, rather than trusting that the gifts of friendship, which were sufficient before, are sufficient still.

Such simple gifts of friendship hold great power for those in need. When talking with someone who has experienced loss, what we need are not new, magic words. Most often, what we should say are some of the old words we may have neglected to speak for a time, or which simply deserve to be said again. These old words still have a lot of magic in them — words like "I'll stay with you," "I love you," and other wordless words that can be quite profound, like an embrace or shared tears.

As I say, often we don't trust that such things are enough. People who have been with friends in need, simply sharing the silence and the tears with them, often leave such encounters saying, "I felt so inadequate. I didn't know what to say. I wish I could have said something or done something." But listen to those who have been on the other end of such an encounter, those who have received such simple, seemingly inadequate expressions of care, and you hear something quite different: "I can't tell you how much that meant. I felt upheld. It made all the difference."

It's hard to know exactly why such simple expressions of care can mean so much. That's a bit of a mystery as well. But I think it has something to do with this: When we share the suffering of a friend — not remove it or explain it, but simply share it — we reflect something of God's love, and God's love can somehow work through us. After all, the God of All Comfort explains little, but loves abundantly and shares our sorrow. God is the One who has the strength and courage and love to wade into the powerful tides of our greatest needs and share our hurt as if it were God's own. And when we do something like that ourselves, we can be instruments of God.

A friend of mine tells of picking up his daughter from kindergarten. She was late in coming out of the classroom. When she finally appeared, she explained to her father why she was delayed. It seems that her friend had worked very hard on a plaster figure that she was looking forward to giving to her parents, but in her excitement she hurried to put on her coat, and the plaster figure dropped to the floor and shattered into many pieces. The father said, "So you stayed to help her pick up the pieces? That was nice of you." "No, Dad," she replied, "I stayed to help her cry."

Now that's a friend.

BEFORE THE CHILD

Luke 1:46-56

EFORE THE CROWDED INN, before the chorus of angels, before the star, before the shepherds and the wise men, even before the child, there was the mother, who wasn't much more than a child herself, receiving word that she was to give birth to a child, to bring forth new life. She also received word that in some way through that child she was to give birth to the whole world and bring new life to all.

Every mother is not only a witness to miracle, but also in some way a part of the miracle. But this mother was part of two miracles: the miracle of a new human life that stirred inside her, and the miracle that in some special way God resided there as well. We can only wonder which miracle more occupied Mary's heart and mind, but I'm quite sure that each miracle would have the power to prompt both fear and praise. Considered together, the two miracles couldn't help but make this simple country girl shudder with the fearsome wonder of it all.

We don't know much about who the angel Gabriel was or is, and we can only imagine how he made himself known to Mary. But this, I think, we can say: He wasn't very subtle, even for an angel. He found Mary and got right down to business, with words that might startle a young woman even if they didn't come from an angel: "Hail, O favored one, the Lord is with you! Blessed are you among women!"

Maybe if you're an angel, you know there's no way to ease into a conversation with a human being, so you don't even try. Or perhaps Gabriel was so fluttering with the news he had come to share that he couldn't contain himself, like a winged obstetrician on his first case who is as eager and nervous as the parents are. So if, as the Bible records, Mary was greatly troubled at the greeting she received, we don't have to wonder why.

And then Gabriel, perhaps seeing the reaction he had stirred, quickly added, "Do not be afraid." It was an appropriate reassurance to one who had just seen an angel. And it was also an appropriate reassurance to a young woman who was about to receive the news that she would soon become a young mother. "Do not be afraid" is, I'm sure, a phrase that is often heard in the offices of earthly obstetricians. "Do not be afraid," even though you don't know what lies ahead. "Do not be afraid," even though you feel more like your mother's child than like a child's mother. "Do not be afraid," even though there's nothing in human experience that can prepare you for this moment.

"Blessed are you among women," said Gabriel. But that may have been an unnecessary addition to the greeting, for young mothers can feel especially blessed without any prompting from man, woman, or angel. "Blessed are you among women," because you are about to witness a miracle, and to be part of a miracle. "Blessed are you among women," because though the cycle of birth is as old as life, it is now to be renewed in you.

But also, "Blessed are you among women" in other ways too. "Blessed are you" in all the ways that God blesses people, not always through pleasure and prosperity, but also, perhaps especially, in the midst of sorrow and trial. God's blessing is also God's burden. The blessing is life in its fullness, and that is also the burden. It is the burden of life in all of its pain and complexity, and in no life would that be more evident than in the life of Mary's child. The seeds of sorrow and trial were as surely in Mary's womb as was this new life. A mother, especially this mother of this child, must be prepared to give birth to both life and death, both joy and pain, for no life is without this uneasy mixture. To receive this blessing is to affirm life in spite of all its contradictions and limits and disappointments. And so, to receive this blessing is ultimately an act of faith.

There are Christian traditions that praise Mary as the one who loved Jesus more than any other person ever did or ever could. And there may be good reason to believe that. It does seem that no love for Jesus could be more remarkable than this love she had for him before his birth, for it was true unconditional love. After all, what love could be more unconditional than love that did not yet know what it would be loving? *Will he be tall or short? Will he be handsome or plain? Will he be attentive or cold? Will he reject me or love me in return?* Somehow, in this miracle of unconditional love, such questions are not asked and need no answer. The love is love of the unknown, a personal devotion to another before that other is more than just a stirring and a promise.

In this way, Mary's experience was not too unlike that of other women in other times and other places, women who learn that they are to give birth and respond with fear, and feel blessed, and who love their unborn child with an unconditional love.

Yet, in other ways, Mary's experience was as far from common human experience as was the very life of Jesus. We can only imagine — and then only dimly — what it would have been like for Mary to know that the child she carried in her womb was also, in some way, at the same time, her parent, as

God is the parent of us all, and thus even the parent of the one who would give him human life.

And though every mother wants to know what kind of child she carries in her womb, how can we imagine receiving the word that Mary received: "He will be great," Gabriel said. Though every parent might think that would be most gratifying news, the message quickly gathered such power that even a mother's imagination could no longer keep up with it. "And he will be called the Son of the Most High; and the Lord God will give to him the throne of his father David, and he will reign over the house of Jacob forever; and of his kingdom there will be no end."

Such news could have been cause for sheer dread, and I'm sure dread was at least part of what Mary felt. And yet, whatever dread there might have been was also coupled with faith and trust. We can catch only a glimmer of what this must have been like. Other mothers may recognize that though a child is their child, the world also lays claim to that same child. Other mothers may know that their desire to protect their child should not prevent the child from claiming his or her destiny. But to have so great a burden laid on one's child, a burden so complete and uncompromising that it doesn't even wait for the child to be born, much less wait for the child to grow older and stronger, why, that requires something else from a mother — a faith and a trust that are almost as much a miracle as the birth itself.

And the story of Mary is different from any of our stories in another way. It is common for us to see God at work in something exotic or distant or dim. It can be more difficult, however, to find God in the familiar and everyday. We may be willing to concede that God has acted in some remembered point in history, but it can be more difficult to affirm that God is acting today. We may grant that God is active in human lives generally, but, ironically, it is often God's actions in our own lives that are most difficult to trace. Our own days are too common, our own lives too familiar for us to sense the mystery of God pulse within them. We who may find it difficult to imagine that God could be somehow uniquely at work in the life of one man at one point in history — we can't even imagine what it would be to know that man as a mother knows a son and still be able to affirm the wild miracle of it.

Mary could look at Jesus with a mother's sure familiarity — every hair on his head, every crease in his face, every turn of his smile. He was as familiar to her as the way home, as close as her own skin. And yet, she could see God there too, not only a God she could love, but also a God she could worship, and a God to whom she could entrust her life.

From Mary we learn something about miracles and how to receive them. Mary understood that God is at work in unexpected places, in the life of a simple country girl through the promise of a child, and from her we can learn that God can be at work in perhaps the most unexpected place of all: our own lives. After all, God's miracles are nowhere more difficult to see than when they occur in front of our eyes.

Before the crowded inn, before the chorus of angels, before the star, before the shepherds and the wise men, even before the child, there was the mother, who wasn't much more than a child herself, receiving word that she was to give birth to a child, bring forth new life, and also receiving word that in some way through that child she was to give birth to the whole world and bring new life to all.

Mary received the promise of the angel as a promise from God and thus in some way as a promise already fulfilled. And, indeed, in time, the child was born, the Son of the Most High. It was a promise fulfilled first in the heart of one young woman, awaiting fulfillment in history. And for us the order has been reversed. The promise has already been fulfilled in history, and now it awaits fulfillment in our hearts.

SAYING GOOD-BYE

Deuteronomy 33:1-5, 26-27; 2 Corinthians 13:11-14

I N MY RECENT READINGS OF THE BIBLE, I have been struck by
how full it is of partings. Even more striking is how different some of those partings are from the ones we usually
make. Many of us are uncomfortable with partings, so often
we fumble through them.

We might try avoidance, perhaps saying to ourselves, *What
could I say? I don't even know what to say.* And so we don't
address the parting — either in our words or in our hearts.

Or we make false promises: "I'm sure we'll have a chance
to talk again before you leave. And we'll see each other again
soon. It's not like you're going very far." None of that may turn
out to be true, but we say it anyway.

And sometimes we can be so uncomfortable with parting
that we redirect our emotions by getting angry, or picking a
fight, or withdrawing entirely.

It's easy to identify some of the reasons why we have dif-
ficulty with good-byes. For one, we doubt that we'll have
the right words for the occasion. But if we do find the right
words, that makes it difficult too, because a parting, once
acknowledged and expressed, can no longer be ignored. To
offer words of parting is to make the painful reality all the
more real, and who wants to do that? And, of course, to say

good-bye is to close a chapter. To be sure, there will be other chapters ahead, but not this chapter, not ever again.

It is in parting that we confront our limits. We cannot be both here and there. We cannot be with all the people we care about. We cannot stop time. We cannot begin to write a new chapter without turning the page.

And there is another way in which we confront our limits in parting. All of our relationships seem incomplete, and it is in parting that we realize that they will always remain that way. Before the time of parting we can say to one another, or just think to ourselves, "Someday soon we'll get together for lunch." Or, "Someday we'll sit down together, and I'll tell you everything that's been going on in my life that I've never known how to begin to tell you." Or, "Someday I'll finally tell you all that you have meant to me." But often that someday never arrives, and at the time of parting we confront that it never will. Good-byes always seem premature because, this side of heaven, even the fullest of lives and the richest of relationships are fragmentary and incomplete.

By contrast, many of the partings in the Bible are tended to with great care and lingered over. They are marked with unblinking honesty, without a trace of denial in sight.

I think of Moses, who led his people out of exile and wandered with them in the wilderness for forty years, who finally reached the verge of the Promised Land, so close that he could see it. It was then and there, before this journey they had shared was complete, that Moses gathered the people of Israel to say good-bye to them. And he took quite a while to do it, saying something to the heads of each tribe. He talked directly about his leaving without a hint of avoidance, without false promises, because he said that the most unavoidable reality of all — the reality of God — would go with them, and the promises Moses related were the changeless promises of God. For Moses and his people, the journey was not complete.

Their dreams still lay in fragments at their feet. But Moses said to them, "And yet . . ." To be sure, he told them, you're still homeless, *and yet* "the eternal God is your dwelling place." We must part, we can no longer cling to one another, *and yet* "underneath it all are the everlasting arms" of God. For Moses, in other words, parting was an occasion to remind one another of the eternal presence and promises of God.

Then, too, I think of Jesus, who didn't avoid the pain of parting by merely slipping away. In fact, the final third of John's Gospel consists largely of Jesus' parting words to his disciples. They didn't want to hear all that he had to say, but Jesus explained, "These things I have spoken to you, while I am still with you. But the Counselor, the Holy Spirit, whom the Father will send in my name, he will teach you all things, and bring to your remembrance all that I have said to you. Peace I leave with you; my peace I give to you; not as the world gives do I give to you. Let not your hearts be troubled, and neither let them be afraid." Jesus knew what the disciples would soon learn: parting is not the time for easy reassurances and false promises. Rather, it is the time to turn again to the assurance of God's continued presence and the promise that even in parting we are gathered up together into the peace of God.

And there was Paul, who, through all of his travels from church to church, had much practice in saying good-bye. He knew that the way he traveled was treacherous, so each time he left a particular community of faith, and each time he closed a letter, he was aware that it might be the last. That's why he always offered his parting words with a sense of urgency, and yet he took his time, to give his heart room to share the breadth of his thought and the depth of his feeling.

When Paul closed his final letter to the church in Corinth, that difficult and recalcitrant church he had loved into being through his blood, sweat, toil, and tears, he left them with some final instructions, and then he said, "Finally, brothers and sisters, farewell. Mend your ways, heed my appeal, agree with one another, live in peace, and the God of love and peace be with you. Greet one another with a holy kiss. And the saints greet you. The grace of the Lord Jesus Christ and the love of God and the fellowship of the Holy Spirit be with you all."

Paul could bring himself to say good-bye to this church only by recognizing that he was not leaving them alone, but leaving them in the grace, love, and fellowship of God — the same God who went with Paul, uniting them even in parting; the same God who drew them together even as they said good-bye; the same God who could complete the work that they had begun when they were together by promising to be with them always, even when they were absent, one from another.

Over and over in Scripture we read of people who, in parting, remind one another of the promises of God. And what other way are we to part — in what other ways *can* we part? How else can we leave those we care about unless we entrust them to the care of God? How else can we look at all the things we haven't had time or ability to say or do, all the broken fragments of our relationships, unless we ask God to gather them up and somehow make them whole, to complete whatever we were not able to complete, and heal whatever we were not able to heal?

That is, after all, what the word *good-bye* means — "God be with you." What else can we say at parting that doesn't simply wither and fall at our feet as soon as it is said?

God be with you, because I can no longer be with you.

God be with you, because though now we will have limited ways of expressing care for one another, we are still — all of us — in need of care.

God be with you, because if God is with you and with me, somehow we will be together still.

God be with you, because though none of our lives is much more than a collection of fragments, some of them with jagged edges, God promises to make them complete and make us whole, in God's time.

Indeed, there may be no way to part from those we love without either kidding ourselves or being drawn into the shadow of despair, unless we say, "Good-bye. God be with you."

WHISPERED IN YOUR EAR

Matthew 3:13-17

WHO WHISPERED IN YOUR EAR when you were very young? Whose whispering voice do you still hear even now, lo, these many years later? Who whispered in your ear and told you who you are in a way that helped shape the person you would become? And what did that whispering voice say?

As soon as a Muslim baby is born, the *adhān* — the call to prayer — is whispered into the baby's right ear. It begins, *Allahu Akbar* — which means "Allah is great" or "God is great." So the word *God* is the first word a baby hears, whispered in her right ear as soon as she is born. And this is the same call to prayer that's issued five times a day. In Muslim areas it echoes through the streets in a haunting chant. Wherever you are, whatever you're doing, the call to prayer finds you and, if you are Muslim, it is a reminder of what was first whispered in your ear when you were born:

> *Allah is great, Allah is great.*
> *I bear witness that there is none worthy of worship but Allah.*
> *I bear witness that Muhammad is the Messenger of Allah.*
> *Hasten to the prayer, hasten to the prayer.*
> *Hasten to real success, hasten to real success.*

Allah is great, Allah is great.
There is none worthy of worship but Allah.

After that is whispered in the baby's right ear, the command to rise and worship is whispered in the baby's left ear. The command is the same as the *adhān*, but with the added phrase "Prayer is ready, prayer is ready." So when a Muslim child is born, the first word she hears in her right ear, and then in her left, is the whispered name of God in a call to prayer and a call to worship. It strikes me as a powerful way of honoring God and binding a child to God in the very first moments of life.

So who whispered in your ear when you were very young? Whose whispering voice do you still hear even now, lo, these many years later? Who whispered in your ear and told you who you are in a way that helped shape the person you would become? And what did that whispering voice say?

Jesus was an adult when he came to the waters of the Jordan to be baptized by John, but in Matthew's Gospel the story is told almost as if it is a second birth narrative. Before this story, Jesus does not speak. He does not act, either, at least not in any way that Matthew found worth recording. But when Jesus emerged from the baptismal waters, dripping like an infant fresh from the womb, the Spirit of God descended upon him and a voice from heaven said, "You are my Son, the Beloved; my favor rests on you."

How different it would be if this declaration of God's favor occurred later in Jesus' life. It would sound very different if it were said only after Jesus had healed the sick, embraced the outcast, and preached good news to the poor. It would be very different because then we might conclude that God's favor was upon him because of all he had done, that in some way Jesus had earned the blessing. Instead, Jesus was immersed in God's favor before he had an opportunity to say anything or do anything. The very first words that Jesus heard as he emerged from the womb of baptism were like words whispered in a baby's ear: "You are my Son, the Beloved; my favor rests on you."

Perhaps that is the voice, and perhaps those are the words, that Jesus continued to hear throughout his life. To love so completely, as Jesus did, he had to have known that he was completely loved. I imagine that he held those words, and the blessing they conveyed, very close, in every hour, especially when events turned hard and people turned away and the cries of the crowd turned nasty — perhaps then he would hear again the words of love still echoing in his ears: "You are my Son, the Beloved; my favor rests on you." How else would he have been able to respond to hostility and betrayal with love, unless he felt so loved himself, in whatever circumstance still drenched with love and soaking in love, the love that declared, "You are my Son, the Beloved; my favor rests on you."

In some ways, of course, it was a unique blessing. When God called Jesus "my Son," it spoke of the unique relationship that Jesus has with the one he called his "Abba," his "Papa." But Scripture also affirms that, through Jesus, we are all drawn into an intimate relationship with God, so that now we are all children of God. So what was said to Jesus when he was baptized is the same that could be said to anyone when they are baptized: "You are my child, my beloved; my favor rests on you."

It can be difficult to hear that voice. There are a lot of other voices out there — the voices of friends, family members, and strangers, the voices of the culture at large — that speak with an amplified voice that is impossible to escape. The voice that calls you "beloved" can be all but drowned out by those other voices that may say very different things, like "You're nothing special," "You're worthless," "You're nobody," "You don't matter, not really."

There are still other voices that also make it difficult for us to hear the voice that calls us "beloved," and, ironically, those are the voices of praise, saying things like "You're an excellent student," "You're going to go places," "You're a good father," "You're a gifted teacher." And the voices keep praising: "You're such a good listener," "Your children are so polite," "You're always there for other people," "You have a lot to be proud of." Obviously, we all need praise on occasion, and we all need to offer praise as well. But words of praise can make it harder for us to hear the voice that calls us "beloved." After all, to be praised and to be beloved are very different things.

Praise is something we earn. We have to do something exemplary to be praised. And if we seek praise often enough and receive it eagerly enough, it can come to seem as if everything — even love — must be earned. If we seek praise often enough and receive it eagerly enough, we can get the impression that to be valued we must do something, preferably something special, and to keep receiving praise we must keep doing more.

So the person who is motivated by praise is quite different from the one who feels assured that he is beloved, or she is beloved. To be called "beloved" is not something that can be earned. It is a gift. There is nothing you have to do to be beloved; there is nothing you *can* do to be beloved. You are God's beloved not because of what you do, but simply because you are God's beloved. Even before you've had a chance to do anything that could be called special, God whispers in your ear, "This is my child, the beloved, in whom I am well pleased."

But it's hard to hear that voice sometimes. In fact, I believe that one of the reasons we're so determined to distinguish ourselves in some way is that we cannot hear that voice. Being special, different, a cut above is the only way we know to keep from being lost in the crowd. We're afraid of feeling forgotten, of going unnoticed.

And we'll do almost anything to distinguish ourselves as special. All the praise we seek. All the recognition. The trophy. The degree. The office. The job. The promotion. The address. The accomplishment of our children. All the ways we endeavor to stand out, to enlarge the scope of our lives. All the ways we use to assure ourselves that we matter, that we have a place in the world, that we are loved. All because we assume we have to do something to be valued.

Over the years I've wondered what it was like when I was first learning to walk. I imagine it went something like this: I stood at one end of the room, with my mother behind me and my father a full three steps away. Before that day I could probably do the kind of creative dangling that almost looks like walking, when somebody held me by the hands and shifted me from side to side as my feet barely touched the floor. But this was the day when I would try a real honest walk on my own — all holds barred — with just two eager parents there to cheer me on. So I set out, wobbling at first, stumbling at second, but unmistakably making it on my own from one set of arms to the other. And then I imagine that my father lifted me high in the air with an exultant shout, as if no one in human history had ever walked before. Then, after numerous kisses and exclamations, I probably felt like the most loved, most marvelous boy in all the world.

After a time I could walk with more assurance, but, for some reason, I didn't receive so much praise. In fact, I couldn't remember the last time that anyone praised me for walking across a room. So I had to do other things. Simply walking just wasn't enough anymore. I had to strive to make a splash in other ways, just to get back to that feeling — that feeling of being noticed, of being picked up with a shout of delight, of being valued.

And in all that striving it was easy to lose sight of the fact that my parents didn't praise me because of my accomplishments. Rather, they praised my accomplishments because they loved me, and would have loved me if there were no accomplishments to praise.

A woman of great accomplishment once confided that she felt as if she had to have her name in the newspaper on a regular basis to be noticed by her parents. She thought she had to do something to earn their love. Only recently has she come to see that her striving didn't increase their love, that she didn't have to do anything noteworthy to be noticed by them, that she didn't have to do anything special to be special to them. For the most part, we don't have much experience with unconditional love, so we try to create conditions in which we'll feel worthy of love. We don't trust love without reasons, so we strive to forge reasons for the love received.

If parents sometimes have something like unconditional love, a love without reasons, for their children, how much more so does God love God's children? In the eyes of God, all of our striving for distinction is so unnecessary. It's trying to win something that is ours already. God values you not because you have distinguished yourself in some way, but because you are God's beloved. You don't have to take those stumbling baby steps, much less change the world, for God to love you.

Many people may have whispered in your ear when you were very young. You may still hear some of their voices, lo, these many years later, telling you who you are in a way that shaped the person you would become. Some of those voices are probably encouraging, while other voices you may have spent much of your life trying to silence. But before all of those voices, and above all of those voices, is the one voice that, before you could do anything or say anything to distinguish yourself in any way, said, "This is my child, my beloved; my favor rests on you." That voice gets drowned out a lot because of the kind of world we live in, because of the kind of people we are.

That is one reason why we worship — to be reminded, in some way, to hear that voice again, to hear from the one who calls us "beloved." We come to worship to silence, for a time, all the distracting and detracting voices, so that the Spirit of the Living God might whisper again in our ears, "You are my beloved." We listen for that word week after week, not just so that we might receive it as a blessed assurance, but so that we might then be equipped to love others. To hear and truly know that we are the beloved of God — this in its own way equips us to serve better than the most impassioned call to action. To love others, as Jesus did, first we are reminded that we are loved, and have been before the beginning, even as Jesus was.

BORN AGAIN?

John 3:1-15

I HAVE BEEN ASKED THE QUESTION a number of times, but the time I remember most clearly happened when I was in divinity school. I was waiting in a dingy little room for snow tires to be put on my car, and I was poring over a theological tome entitled *Evil and the God of Love*. It's definitely the kind of book you read with two hands. It has the weight of a millstone, complete with hefty quotations from the likes of Anselm and Augustine. The woman next to me asked what I was reading, so I told her as best I could, trying to play down the part about Anselm and Augustine. When she looked puzzled, I explained that I was a student in divinity school.

Then she asked me, "Are you born again?"

I've been asked that question a number of times since, but I think this was the first time, so my mind raced, searching for an answer that would speak for me and speak to her. How do you begin to answer a question like that?

I also remember having the distinct impression that she was looking for a simple "yes" or "no." It was time to show my union card, if I had one. I didn't know how she viewed herself, but she wanted to know if I was one of "us" or one of "them." I wanted to tell her that I was "born again" in the sense that God is more to me than a mere abstraction from a theological book, that God had changed my life, that Jesus Christ is a living reality to me, that I rely on the Holy Spirit, but that I have never had the kind of conversion experience that is usually implied when the term "born again" is used. My faith experience has unfolded over time. It didn't come on a particular day in a particular place. I couldn't point to any birthday in the faith and say, "That's the day I was born again."

But how do you say all of that in a crowded, dingy little room, waiting for snow tires to be put on your car?

So I settled for saying, "Yes, I am born again, but maybe not in the way you're talking about."

Not missing a beat, she said, "I mean it in the way Jesus meant it," and then she pulled out a little Bible from her purse and read from John's Gospel: "Truly, truly I say to you, unless one is born anew, he cannot see the kingdom."

I don't know how the conversation would have continued if I hadn't been called to pick up my car. As it was, we simply said good-bye. As I drove back to school, I was reminded of George Bernard Shaw's observation that Americans and Britons are divided by a common language. How true that can be of Christians. Sometimes it seems that we're divided by a common faith, and often the division has come with this question. Today, when polls are taken in advance of an election, there's a category of "born again" voters. Those who see themselves as born again are now viewed as a voting bloc.

The term "born again" derives from a passage in the Gospel of John. That passage is the source of the controversy, and yet, at the same time, one of the ways to get beyond the controversy is found in that same passage. Indeed, it's ironic that this passage and this concept of being born again have become divisive, because Jesus intended his words to achieve precisely the opposite effect. They were meant to be inclusive rather than exclusive. They were intended to draw together rather than to divide.

It begins with a man named Nicodemus, who comes to see Jesus at night — which is fitting, because he's in the dark. He has a question, and he wants to be enlightened by Jesus. That in itself is remarkable because Nicodemus, a Pharisee, is used to being the answerer, not the asker, of questions. As a Pharisee, he was a scrupulous keeper of the law, a pillar of the synagogue, a respected religious leader. No wonder he comes to see Jesus at night — he doesn't want anyone to see him seeking guidance from an untutored teacher from a backwater town.

For Nicodemus, as for all Pharisees, religion was almost a family business, not in the sense that sons of Pharisees and grandsons of Pharisees often decided to become Pharisees themselves, but in a more direct sense: being a Pharisee was something that was handed down from generation to generation as one might pass down the royal crown or the family name. One's status as a Pharisee was assumed and automatic. There was no element of choice involved. You were born a Pharisee. And not only was the status handed down, but the Pharisees assumed that their heritage included — simply by the fact of their birth — special access to God and special understanding of God's ways.

So when Jesus tells Nicodemus that he must be born again, he is saying, in part, that being born into the Pharisaic tradition isn't enough. You have to be born in a different way, in a spiritual way. You have to experience God and accept God for yourself as an individual, and citing your pedigree just isn't enough. By putting this emphasis on the new life in faith, Jesus is saying that we all start on an even footing. There is no privilege of birth where God is concerned, because the kind of birth God cares about is the birth of spirit in which we can all take part.

Notice that this is such a revolutionary concept for Nicodemus that he's more than a little slow to grasp it. Old ways of thinking are slow to leave us. So Nicodemus asks Jesus, "How can an old codger like me be born spanking new like a baby? Can someone enter the mother's womb a second time?" In other words, Nicodemus is still thinking in physical terms, about physical birth, because that's the way he's used to thinking — that religious faith and position are a privilege of birth. Now Jesus is saying that something else is required. You've got to have a second, different kind of birth, a birth of faith and devotion that isn't an automatic by-product of your ancestry.

Jesus' contention that a Pharisee has no special access to God because of his birth is meant to be inclusive, to validate the experience of those who aren't Pharisees but who love and serve God nonetheless. Not everyone can be born a Pharisee. But anyone can have another kind of birth, a spiritual birth, and that's what really counts.

But see what has happened in our day. Jesus' words have been twisted around to exclude where Jesus would include, for recently the term "born again" has been used by some to say that everyone must have the same kind of spiritual experience, the experience of a dramatic conversion, for their faith to be true and real. Why is it that we humans always seem to want to exclude others? Why do we insist upon separating the sheep from the sheep? There's another way to put it: Why won't we let God deal with each person as God sees fit?

God is like a good doctor. God doesn't prescribe the same medicine for everyone. But some turn that around and insist that the way God works in our life or the life of another is the only way God can work.

This kind of mistrust and division has come from both sides, from both the so-called born-again Christians and Christians who have grown up in the faith without experiencing a conversion.

For instance, sometimes the "born again" Christian can act

a lot like a young man who has just fallen head-over-heels in love for the first time. During the first flush of love, he visits his grandparents, who have been married for forty-five years. As he's sitting with his grandfather at the breakfast table, the young lover says to his grandfather, "Don't you just get all tingly inside every time grandmother walks into the room?"

His grandfather looks over his shoulder at his wife, who's cooking bacon. "Well . . . ," replies the grandfather, not wanting to disappoint the boy, "yes, sometimes. . . . Yes, I think I know what you mean."

"Don't you get almost light-headed thinking about her?"

The grandfather pauses. "Light-headed? Well, not exactly light-headed."

The grandson is disappointed. His experience of young love is so strong that he can't see that other, different experiences can also be valid. What the young lover has failed to learn is that there are many signs of devotion, and that the kind of enthusiasm he has come to know is only one of them. There is also constancy. There is continued service. There is devotion through the waves of circumstance and the tides of time. There are all the quieter satisfactions of life and love that are no less real, but that are without the bold gestures of young love.

It seems to me that sometimes the "born again" Christian can likewise fail to appreciate the expressions of faith in those who haven't had a dramatic conversion. In fact, the "born again" Christian can even go so far as to doubt that such a faith can be real, because it doesn't resemble his or her own experience.

Just as there are many ways to express love, so there are many ways to express faith. If the Apostle Paul were alive today, he probably would be called a "born again" Christian. After all, he was struck down on the road to Damascus in an encounter with God that was the quintessential conversion experience. It was all there: the heavens cracked open like a walnut, a blinding light, a life turned upside down and then turned around, a specific date and time when he accepted Christ. Paul was a convert, and his letters burn with a convert's characteristic zeal.

But there are others, the original twelve disciples among them, who never had such an experience. Their faith grew over time, and yet even Paul, the great convert, recognizes their experience as valid and their faith as real.

Again, God is like a good doctor. A good doctor doesn't prescribe the same medicine for everyone. Gradual growth and dramatic turnarounds come from the same God, who deals with each of us individually.

There's also a lesson that those of us who haven't had a dramatic conversion experience can learn from those who have had such an experience. It's really the same lesson that Nicodemus learned from Jesus, and it's this: Being born into a particular family or into a particular tradition does not, in itself, make you a Christian. Saying that you are a Christian is more than saying that you are not Jewish, or Buddhist, or Muslim. It's more than a way to divide people in a national census.

For instance, my family tree is laden with enough Christian ministers to make that poor tree bend to the ground under the weight of us all. Knowing this, and nothing else, you might be tempted immediately to assume that I too am a Christian. That would be the correct assumption if one becomes a Christian in the same way one becomes an American citizen — simply by being born here.

We sometimes forget that, in addition to growing up in the faith, there is an element of decision that is essential and, in my "mainline Protestant" tradition, so easily lost. After all, our tradition doesn't usually include dramatic altar calls or impassioned calls for conversion.

In my tradition, we tend not to emphasize decision. Instead, we talk about growth in faith. Eventually, however, each person must stand before his or her God and say either "Yea" or "Nay." We can put so much emphasis on growth in faith that we run the danger of never putting forth the most crucial question: "Are you committed to Christ? Will you decide for him today?"

People sometimes object that, in religious matters, the language of decision is too confining to reflect the ambiguity of our experience. Such language can seem so black-and-white when our experience of God often is in a shade of gray. Many students prefer "true or false" questions on a test because even if they have absolutely no idea which is the correct answer, they still have an even chance of guessing it correctly. But in religious matters, a true/false, either/or decision can be discomforting. The decision seems too absolute, the choices too few. In matters of faith, when faced with the need for decision, we're tempted to ask, "Don't you have any essay questions?" We want to be able to qualify our answers. We want to be able to say, "Yes, but on the other hand. . . ."

So we talk about growth in faith. We may not be ready to decide, but we are willing to grow. We use images like "pilgrimage" and "spiritual journey." Instead of arriving at a decision, we can see ourselves as perpetually en route.

If we emphasize either decision or growth to the virtual exclusion of the other, we are posing a false choice. Both decision and growth have a place in relationships, including our relationship with God. This is easy to observe in matters of the heart. There is a place for the slow flowering of love, but there is also a place for the decision to marry. Likewise, in our relationship with God, there is a place for the slow growth of faith, but there is also a place for decision. Growth and decision are not unrelated. Growth in faith can lead to decision. And, too, it can be in living out the implications of our commitment to God, our decision to follow Jesus, that our faith can best grow and flourish.

This is some of what I wanted to tell the woman in that dingy little room as we waited to have snow tires put on our cars, but I never had a chance. So now I have told you.

WHO'S THAT KNOCKING
AT MY DOOR?

Revelation 3:15-22

THE RULE OF BENEDICT IS A DOCUMENT that has ordered the life of Benedictine monks for 1,500 years. That remarkable document, written by Saint Benedict of Nursia, instructs the monks in how they are to live their daily lives together in community. One of the things that Benedict describes in the Rule is a particular role, that of the "porter" of the monastery. Quite simply, the porter is the one who opens the door to the monastery when someone knocks. Not much of a role, you say? Ah, but there's so much to it — so much entailed and so much communicated in how one opens a door. Roman Catholic nun and author Joan Chittister goes so far as to say, "The way we answer doors is the way we deal with the world."[1]

So in the Rule of Benedict, the porter is given very specific instructions. He is to sleep near the entrance to the monastery so he can hear and respond in a timely way when someone knocks. Then, as soon as anyone knocks, likely a poor person (because they often sought refuge in monasteries), the porter is to reply, "Thanks be to God. Your blessing, please." He is to

---

1. Joan Chittister, *The Rule of Saint Benedict* (New York: Crossroad Publishing, 1992), p. 284.

say this before he even knows who's on the other side of the door. Before the porter knows who that person is or why he or she is there, he is to praise God for that person's presence and to ask for his or her blessing.

Dorothy Parker, an author famous for her dark wit, used to answer her telephone with this greeting: "What fresh hell is this?" Most of us don't respond in that way, but I do know a pastor who says that when he started in ministry, when he would go into his office and see that little red light on the phone indicating that he had a message, his first response was something like "Uh-oh." He anxiously wondered what need was being brought to him and whether he could meet it. He would have to collect himself a bit before he could pick up the receiver and listen to the message. He's grateful to have gotten over that response, but I don't think he's gotten to the point of seeing that little red light on the phone and saying, "Thanks be to God."

What do you think when someone knocks on your door? Is it closer to "What fresh hell is this?" or "Thanks be to God"? Probably somewhere in between, I imagine. But which way do you lean?

Benedict goes on to say that the porter should be prepared to respond whenever there is a knock at the door. It could be in the middle of the night or when the porter has just sat down to eat. The porter is to be welcoming at all times, and not just when it's convenient. The porter is to offer a welcome, in Benedict's words, "with all the gentleness that comes from reverence of God," and "with the warmth of love." And then the porter is to make sure that the other monks know of the presence of a visitor in their midst so that they can join in extending a welcome.

Some communities — perhaps by taking the lead of their official or unofficial porters — radiate a kind of welcome that receives visitors as gifts, no matter the circumstances.

Particularly when you are in need, perhaps nothing is more life-giving than that kind of welcome.

While a student in seminary, I was driving with a couple of friends in the beautiful and genteel countryside of northwestern Connecticut when our car broke down. It was a time before cell phones, so I needed to find a phone. I went up to the nearest house and knocked on the door. I could hear much conversation and laughter coming from the house. The man who opened the door — who had never seen me before — didn't step outside to speak with this stranger, didn't stand in the doorway while I stood outside. Instead, his first words to me were "Please come in." He didn't know me. He didn't know why I was there. But he immediately said, "Please come in." I remember being quite struck by that — taken aback, really.

When I stepped inside and told him about my car problem, he let me use the phone. When I got off the phone, I thanked him, and he asked how long before the roadside-service truck would get there. "They said about half an hour." He responded, "Well then, you might as well join the party. Can I get you a glass of wine?" When I explained that I had two friends back in the car, he said, "Well, bring them in."

So my friends and I joined the party. When the roadside-service truck arrived and the car was revived (as I recall, it just needed some kind of belt), I went back to the house to thank our host. He said, "Oh, but please stay for dinner." Then I noticed that my friends already had plates in their hands. It was as if we were expected all along. By the way, it was soon after we joined the party that we learned that this was a gathering of a Bible study group from the local Episcopal church. That was over thirty years ago. But you don't forget a welcome like that.

Some households are like that. The home in which I grew up was a welcoming one, but my parents always liked to be prepared for visitors. When I was in high school, if I told my mother that a couple of friends were going to come over to, say, watch a hockey game on TV, she would have sodas put out on the kitchen counter, with a bowl of potato chips with plastic wrap over the top to keep them crisp. She would peek in the room where we were watching the game and greet my friends, but not stay very long, which we, as teenage boys, probably thought was just about right. So she had a wonderful welcoming way when she was prepared for guests. But not so much when visitors came unannounced. When, say, one of my friends would just show up, just knock on the door, both of my parents were just a little bit thrown by that. Just a little, but enough that I could sense it, and perhaps my friends could too.

Perhaps that's why in high school we always seemed to gravitate to David Blair's house. That was the gathering place. If you didn't know where my friends and I were, it would be a safe bet that we would be at David's. Why was that? Quite simply, because his parents were like porters. It was like they were always expecting us to knock on the door (when we even bothered to knock on the door). They made it seem like there was no such thing as an inconvenient time, and that our presence wasn't a burden, but more like a gift.

So I think of the porter in the monastery, and the people who play that role in the congregations that I've served, and I think of the host who welcomed three young strangers like treasured guests at his party, and I think of David Blair's parents. And I wonder why more of us aren't like that. I wonder what prevents us from responding to a knock on the door by saying, "Thanks be to God."

To state the obvious, most of us don't like interruptions. We would rather live our days by our own plans. I try to imagine someone asking me, "Could I interest you in an interruption today?" I might respond, "No, thanks. Being interrupted isn't on my list of things to do today."

I say that by way of confession, of course, because I recognize that interruptions are one of God's preferred ways of getting our attention. The origin of the word *interrupt* is helpful here. It is derived from two Latin words: *inter*, meaning "between," and *rumpere*, which means "break in."

We usually experience interruptions as our routine *breaking up*, when it may be that God is trying to *break in* to our lives. Interruptions can be God's way of breaking in between our moments, breaking in between our harried rushing from this to that, breaking in between our rigid expectations. Sometimes a knock on the door is that kind of interruption. And so the porter says in response, "Thanks be to God."

Father Theodore Hesburgh reflected on his experience as the president of the University of Notre Dame by noting that when he started in that role, he was very impatient with students and faculty who, by knocking on his door, were continually interrupting his work. That response lasted until he realized that the interruptions *were* his work. Well, that's not only true of university presidents. It's true of Christians, all of us. Interruptions are our work. "Thanks be to God."

We can have a hard time receiving a knock on the door with immediate thanksgiving because the one who arrives may not be the one we expected. It may be a stranger whose ways are indeed strange to us. That requires something like adjustment. To make room for a guest requires that we adjust our routines and our expectations.

Sometimes the stranger who requires that kind of hospitality is a member of our own family. One father I know, when the contours of his daughter's personality began to emerge, said, "It's like we welcomed a stranger into our house, a stranger who didn't come from the outside, but from the inside." We may be able to choose to have children, but we cannot choose the children we have. Often the one we are asked to receive is not the one we expected. Perhaps that's why the porter doesn't even wait to see who's knocking on the door before declaring, "Thanks be to God." That way it's clear that the word of thanks is offered unconditionally. There is no asking the stranger to change, or be somehow different, before a word of thanksgiving can be offered.

A pastor friend of mine served a church where there was declining membership, so he prayed for new members to enliven his congregation. He asked the members of his congregation to join him in those prayers. Just a few new families — was that too much to ask? The new families he envisioned never came. But a home for adults with developmental disabilities did open nearby, and some of the residents began to come to worship. And then those folks brought some of their friends. The congregation received these newcomers warmly but a bit awkwardly at first. It required something of an adjustment. For one thing, they had to adjust their expectations of what a new member of the church would be like. True hospitality doesn't ask a guest to change, but does demonstrate a willingness to be changed by the guest. When these newcomers joined the church, my friend said that it was the most joyous service they had shared in a very long time. "By receiving these new folks," he told me, "we became more of a church than I thought we were capable of." In other words, they had been changed.

To be sure, we don't always hear a knock on the door and immediately respond, "Thanks be to God." That can be hard to do sometimes. Without implying that the issues surrounding immigration are simple — they are not — I do think it's interesting to think about immigration in this way. When, as it were, an immigrant knocks on our door, is our response more like Dorothy Parker's "What fresh hell is this?" or closer to the porter's "Thanks be to God"?

Why is the porter in a Benedictine monastery so quick to respond when someone knocks on the door? Why does he go to such extraordinary lengths to welcome the stranger? It isn't just out of some general sense that it's the right thing to do. Rather, the porter immediately gets up to respond when someone knocks on the door because it might be Jesus. Not Jesus as we have ever encountered him before, but Jesus just the same. As an old Celtic saying has it, "Oft, oft, oft goes Christ in stranger's guise." Or, as Mother Teresa of Calcutta used to put it, "Jesus often comes to us in his distressing disguise as one of the poor."

After all, didn't Jesus say, "As you did to one of the least of these, my brothers and sisters, you did it to me"?

So when a porter — or someone with a porter's spirit — hears a knock on the door, he doesn't tarry or ask, "Who's that knocking at my door?" Instead, he gets up and declares, "Thanks be to God" and asks, "Your blessing, please," because it could be Jesus. And often — oft, oft, oft — it is.

CHOIR PRACTICE
IN PRISON

Acts 16:25-31

HAVE YOU NOTICED HOW MUCH of our lives is occupied with the telling and hearing of stories?

The meal is over, the dessert plates long since pushed aside, but you and your dinner guests stay around the table, telling stories. Or, your family has gathered for a funeral, and when the shock of the loss begins to melt, there is a flood of stories about the one who is gone.

There are the stories told to a child at bedtime, and the old, worn stories good friends will listen to just one more time. There are the stories that are briefly captured in the newspaper before they're brushed aside by the next day's news, and enduring stories that have been read by generations. All those stories.

The stories that fill our lives are not just ways to pass the time, mere diversions. They have a meaning and a power beyond anything we usually recognize. All stories reveal underlying assumptions about the way the world works, what is important in life and what is not.

Listen to our stories. Who is the villain and who is the hero? Who succeeds and who does not? What is the object of life, and how does it all turn out in the end? The stories we tell give answers to all of those questions, and more. And so, we live by stories, all of us do — not so much by creeds or even by principles as much as by stories. Stories shape our lives, give our lives meaning and direction, energy and inspiration.

In our time, the stories that most occupy us, and may most influence us, are the stories that come to us through the media — through television and, increasingly, through the Internet. These are the stories of our culture, the stories that tell us who we are and what we are to value. They have become a kind of default catechism for our culture. Whether it's a TED talk on YouTube, or a celebrity gossip Web site, or *Mad Men*, or *60 Minutes* — as different as they may be, what they all have in common is that they are brought to us by people who are trying to sell us things. That is, the underlying story that unites them all is the message that we are supposed to learn how to be good consumers. That, it seems, is the purpose of life. That is our duty and our joy.

Rarely is it stated that bluntly. But sometimes it is, as in a bumper sticker I saw a while back, which read: "The one who dies with the most toys wins." It is both shocking and somehow refreshing finally to see it spelled out so starkly. Sometimes that seems to be the dominant story of our culture. Life is a contest, a game, in which the play involves the accumulation of entertaining and diverting possessions.

The question to ask of such a story, or any story we live by, is this: Does it hold up in the end? Does life really work that way? Does getting and spending really produce satisfaction? Let's be honest: it does, up to a point. For instance, if I have had a particularly difficult day, sometimes I can be cheered by simply walking into, say, a kitchen store. And I have a serious Amazon.com habit. How serious? Let's put it this way: I'm on a first-name basis with the UPS driver. Whenever I see him pull over in front of our house, I experience a little jolt of pleasure at the prospect of getting a little package with my name on it. So it works — for a time.

I recently read that the average young person spends almost two hours and forty-six dollars every time he or she goes to a shopping mall. Why? Because it's fun. For some people going shopping is an enjoyable diversion.

But is it a story that is big enough to live by, especially when the tough times come? Can it hold the weight of a human life? It doesn't take a moment's reflection to recognize that it cannot. "The one who dies with the most toys wins" isn't a strong enough narrative to hold the weight of a human life.

For one, such a story isn't idealistic enough. There is no call to sacrifice, to stretch, to live for something higher or deeper.

Then, too, such a story is not realistic enough. The reality is that all the toys, trips, and possessions we can buy cannot carry us successfully through the pains, disappointments, and losses that, sooner or later, will be a part of our lives. They cannot equip us to face the agonies and confusions that will come.

That is why, finally, it is another story that saves, a story that could sustain Paul and Silas in prison (Acts 16:25-31). They were in Philippi for the sole purpose of telling this story. And it got them into trouble because it challenged the story by which some merchants were making a killing in that town. Most people can be quite decent and hospitable until you start messing with their economic interests. Paul and Silas crossed that line, so their clothes were torn off, and then they were badly beaten and thrown into jail.

But how do they react to this experience — the damp stone, the chains, the bruised limbs, the rejection, the defeat of their plans? They hold choir practice. They sing. Their voices echo off the stone walls, fill the jail, and runneth over into the street outside.

Would you do that? Would you sing under those circumstances? Paul and Silas can sing because they live by a story that can be set to music. Their hymns are love songs that tell the story of God's love, a love that can reach into any place and circumstance, even to condemned prisoners chained to the wall of a jail cell. They sing the story of One who entered the dark corners and prisons of our lives so that we can join him in his freedom and victory.

That seems to me a good test of the stories we choose to live by: Can I take this story to prison with me? Would it sustain me even then? Other stories may be sufficient when life is gentler and brighter. But what story will hold up to reality when life is hard and rough?

If we have the right story, the songs will come. After all, only some stories can be set to music. I doubt, for instance, that the line "The one who dies with the most toys wins" will ever become a popular song lyric. We will not soon hear hymns to self-interest and rising net worth. Don't look for a new hymn titled "Joyful, Joyful, We Adore Ourselves" any time soon.

There are many stories that simply won't fly as songs. It is as if the music refuses to carry stories that are unworthy. I once saw an interview with a songwriter who had written hundreds of songs. He was asked to name one of them that wasn't in some way about love. He was stumped! He couldn't think of one. So many of our songs, of whatever genre, are about love. Love is a story that can be set to music.

But not all stories and songs about love are sufficient in every circumstance. My wife, Karen, and I once celebrated our anniversary by spending the evening in the Rainbow Room, atop Rockefeller Center in Manhattan. Even if you've never visited the Rainbow Room, I'm sure you've seen it in movies from the thirties and forties. It is everyone's picture of an Art Deco nightclub, the tables set in tiers around a revolving circular dance floor, a big band playing, and the lights of Manhattan providing the backdrop for the whole scene. It was a wonderful evening. I don't usually enjoy activities that make me feel inept — but dancing is an exception. Fred

Astaire is one of my idols. It has always seemed to me that he is an enduring icon of grace. In fact, in my dreams I *am* Fred Astaire. I mean that quite literally. I'm Fred Astaire, and my dancing is as light and effervescent as the bubbles in a glass of champagne (but, alas, only in my dreams).

The music that night was strictly George and Ira Gershwin, Cole Porter, and the like — all about love, of course. Everything seemed to fit: the occasion, the setting, the music, the words about love filling the air.

But then the band played one song that transported me to a different time and place, a funeral service I had attended a few months before. The person who died had loved the old standards and requested that a few of her favorites be sung at her funeral. And one of the songs that was sung was the same song to which couples were twirling around the dance floor in the Rainbow Room — "Love Is Here to Stay" by the Gershwin brothers. It's a beautiful, romantic ballad: "In time the Rockies may crumble, Gibraltar may tumble, they're only made of clay, but our love is here to stay."

I love that song. And I loved listening to it in the Rainbow Room, but I found it painful at the memorial service. Now, don't think I'm being a grump here. I'm not so much concerned about such music disrupting the decorum of a funeral. But, you see, it just didn't hold up to the occasion. In the Rainbow Room, where life is sparkling and bright, such romantic sentiments are sufficient. By contrast, at the funeral, in the midst of harsher realities, we need something more. In the face of such a grim and powerful reality, a ballad about romantic love just seems to blow away like a frail flower in a stiff, cold wind.

I adore the kind of love songs that are sung at the Rainbow Room. But we also need a different kind of love song, the kind that can be sung in the dark corners of our lives, at the funerals and in the prison cells.

A few years ago, a Greek cruise ship sank off the coast of South Africa. Soon after the ship ran aground in a severe storm, the crew deserted (with a few passengers) in lifeboats. The remaining passengers were brought into the main dining room to await the rescue helicopters. There the ship's entertainers tried to help keep panic and gloom at bay with magic tricks, jokes, and sing-alongs. One passenger later recalled, "There we were, sitting in the dark, singing songs to keep our minds off the cold and fright. We began with 'We Are Sailing,' but decided it wasn't true. We got into 'My Bonnie Lies over the Ocean' and 'Bye-Bye Love, Bye-Bye Happiness,' but this did nothing for morale."[1]

Eventually all the passengers were saved before the ocean consumed the ship. But I wonder if, since that experience, any of the passengers have searched for other stories to live by, other songs to sing amid the threatening storms that are sure to return.

We sometimes make rather meager claims for the Christian nurture of our children. We say we want to "expose" them to Christian teachings. So we bring them to church school or other church activities in much the way we bring them to soccer practice or dance class, because it's another thing that can help them in their development.

The story of Paul and Silas singing in prison reminds us that faith in the living God, the kind of faith that will be available in a crisis, requires more. You have to come to church to hear this story, and you have to come over and over again for that story to begin to have its way with you. Such a relationship with God has to be patiently nurtured over time. It is a slow, and in some ways demanding, process. Along the way, you may have many occasions to wonder if your efforts

1. Christopher S. Wren, "All 571 aboard Cruise Ship Are Saved," *The New York Times*, August 6, 1991.

are fruitless. You tell your children the story of our God in part so they can draw upon it when the need is great. You pray with them in and out of season in part so that other prayers will not escape them (or us!) when the need is dire.

A crisis is no time to try to introduce ourselves to God. So we dare not approach nurture in the Christian faith lightly or casually; it is serious, urgent stuff. Because the storms will come. They will come eventually.

When you think about it, it's a remarkable thing: There are Paul and Silas in prison, in death's waiting room, singing hymns. That doesn't just happen. In order to be able to sing hymns in prison, you have to have already sung them over and over again, in every circumstance, until they can be sung — in a telling phrase — "by heart." That is, for such songs to be brought into prison, they have to nestle somewhere deep in the heart and take up residence there.

We can be grateful that the story by which Paul and Silas lived was big enough to take to prison with them. It is a story that could be set to music, because it is a love story. But it is a special kind of love story — the story of God's fierce and tireless love for all of God's children.

IT'S ABOUT TIME

Isaiah 40:1-11

ADVENT IS A SEASON IN WHICH we are acutely aware of time. Most of us mark time more intentionally in this season. We may mark the days by opening the little windows of an Advent calendar, or mark the weeks by lighting the candles of an Advent wreath. And if we were ever to lose track of where we are in the month, there are the commercials that relentlessly remind us how many shopping days there are until Christmas.

We have different perceptions of the pace of time in this season. When we're young, December seems to stretch beyond all reason, almost to the dimensions of eternity. When we're young, Advent is a marathon. When we're older, it becomes a sprint. So much to do. So little time.

Our sense of the nature of time is shaped by this season. The repeated patterns and rituals associated with Advent and Christmas can make time seem cyclical. We do the same things year after year. This is what we always eat on Christmas Eve. These are the dishes we always use. This is the grace we always say. This is the story we always tell. This is the song we always sing. Each year Mom always gets everyone a new pair of pajamas. We always laugh when Dad starts cursing as he tries to put up the Christmas tree lights. Gramme always has a glass of tawny port when she gets home from Christmas Eve services. Every year the same things are said or sung, heard or done.

In our family, decorating the tree is a yearly ritual that is so firmly ingrained that it has its own liturgy. There are certain things we always do, and certain things we always say.

First, with help, I put the Christmas tree in the stand and, as I'm doing that, I always complain about the stand. Then my wife, Karen, puts on the lights because she's the only one with enough patience for that task. As she finishes up that job, our children, Alanna and Todd, and I begin to unwrap the ornaments. Many of the ornaments have stories that go along with them, stories we tell every year.

I'll pull out the ornament I made in kindergarten. It's a Styrofoam ball with toothpicks stuck into it that's spray-painted light blue, topped off with silver glitter. Most of its toothpicks have fallen out by now, and much of the glitter is gone too, but I'll invariably comment on its beauty. This is also one of the ornaments that has a name. We call it "Sputnik," because it looks something like that first Russian spacecraft, which was launched about the time I made this ornament. My children love Sputnik and always insist that it be put in the front of the tree where everyone can see it.

Not so with the ornament we have dubbed "Starface." In this ornament the points of the star are made of white fabric, and there is a rosy-cheeked ceramic face in the center. It looks like one of the points of the star is a pointy cap for this cherub. I love Starface. My children, on the other hand, profess a deep hatred of it. Alanna tells me that it used to give her nightmares. Todd's comment is always the same: "It's just disturbing, Dad." Every year he says that.

Another ornament is named "Pinecone Minister," because, well, the face is made of a pinecone, and the body of the ornament is dressed like a minister. We all love Pinecone Minister.

He has wire-rimmed glasses and a wise, gentle look. You trust him. You'd be willing to listen to his sermons even if they were dull, because he's such an endearing person. I'm sure that you, never having met Pinecone Minister, may find this hard to picture. But, believe me, were you to meet him, you would love him too. The very fact that I use the verb "meet" to describe a Christmas ornament tells you a great deal about how we regard him in our family. Every year we affirm our love for him.

Almost every ornament has a story — about the people who gave it to us, or the year that one of us made it, or how someone who is now gone once loved it, or how much we love it and why. And if I forget a part of the liturgy, the story behind some ornament, someone in the family will ask, "Don't you remember?" and then fill in the story. In this way the liturgy is carefully, lovingly preserved. Every year we hang the same ornaments and tell the same stories, as if time itself were cyclical.

A friend of mine likes to tell the story of a new family in her church whose child had only one year of experience in church school. So when it came time to rehearse the Christmas pageant his second year, the boy was aghast: "Do you mean to tell me that we're going to do exactly the same story we did last year?"

Yes, that's what we do. Every year. Exactly the same.

But not exactly.

Time isn't entirely cyclical, is it? Many things may repeat, but something is always different. There's a new person at the table. Or someone is missing. (Doesn't it seem like someone is always missing at Christmas?) Or someone isn't able to play the role she once did. Or the players may be the same, but the relationships have changed. Or time has simply taken its toll. For, as poet Dylan Thomas once observed, "Like a running grave, time tracks you down." Eventually we all get tracked down by time. So it's never the same. Not exactly. I think that's the biggest reason why we're so drawn to nostalgia in this season. Because things change. As writer Ben Hecht once put it, "Time is a circus, always packing up and moving away."

I'm a fan of the television program *Mad Men*. Beginning in the late 1950s, it focuses on an advertising agency on Madison Avenue. The creative director of that agency is Don Draper, a brilliant but troubled man who's keeping an enormous secret about his life. In the first season it's clear that Don drinks too much, and that his family life is a mess. After his repeated infidelities, his marriage is on the verge of disintegrating. Despite these issues, Don tries to focus on his work. One of his clients is the Kodak Company. They've come up with a new slide projector: it has the slides in a wheel instead of in a straight tray. This isn't a big innovation, so they look to Don to come up with an advertising campaign that will make people want this new slide projector.

The clients come into the conference room. "So, have you figured how to work the wheel into it?" they ask.

Don starts in. "Well, technology is a glittering lure. But, uh, there is the rare occasion when the public can be engaged on a level beyond flash, if they have a sentimental bond with the product. My first job I was in-house at a fur company with this old pro copywriter, Greek, named Teddy. Teddy told me that the most important idea in advertising is 'new.' It creates an itch. You just put your product in there like Calamine lotion. But he also talked about a deeper bond with the product. Nostalgia — it's delicate, but potent."

Then Don turns on the slide projector, and as he continues his presentation, he clicks through slides of his family in happier times. In one slide his two children are playing in the backyard. In another his son has fallen asleep on his chest. In another Don is putting his ear to his pregnant wife's belly. In another the two are kissing on New Year's Eve. All the while, he continues with his presentation.

"Teddy told me that in Greek, 'nostalgia' literally means 'the pain from an old wound.' It's a twinge in your heart far more powerful than memory alone." Then, referring to the slide projector, he says, "This device isn't a spaceship; it's a time machine. It goes backwards, and forwards . . . it takes us to a place where we ache to go again. It's not called the wheel; it's called the *carousel*. It lets us travel the way a child travels — around and around, and back home again, to a place where we know we are loved."[1]

And the scene ends with Don silently clicking through more slides of his family in happier times.

My father, who was a minister, always battled melancholy in this season, a melancholy that usually took the form of nostalgia. Although I normally adored spending time with my father, in the days leading up to Christmas he wasn't all that much fun to be with. The bright lights of this season had limited power over the darkness of his moods. Ironically, perhaps, his writing and preaching during Advent and Christmas were always particularly brilliant, probably because he was able to speak to some of the deep longings that we can experience in this season.

Most often, the focus of my father's melancholic nostalgia was on a time when his three children were younger and when his father was still alive. But I wonder: Even when we were younger, did Christmas ever feel complete? Was there ever a time when his heart wasn't traced with longing? You see, there's always someone missing at Christmas. Things are never like they used to be. Not completely. What we long for, I think, is not merely a Christmas from our past, or even some idealized version of it. Instead, I think what we long for is a gathering up of our past, present, and future into a harmony

1. *Mad Men*, 2007, Season 1, Episode 13: "The Wheel." Quoted in www.imdb.com/title/tt1105057/quotes.

that isn't achieved in the days of our lives. What we desire isn't merely to be with those we love, but to be united with them in a way that isn't possible even when they're present. What we yearn for is something we haven't fully seen, something we can't completely imagine, because what we yearn for is God.

My father was a person of great faith, but nostalgia was his temptation. In one way or another, it is for all of us. I call nostalgia a temptation because, although Scripture enjoins us to remember with gratitude, at every turn it also points us to the future. When we read Isaiah's improbable picture of the Peaceable Kingdom that is yet to be, where the wolf lives harmoniously with the lamb, and the lion becomes a vegan, we can only conclude that the good old days, as good as they may have been, are nothing compared to what God has in store for us.

The culture at large tries to drench this season in nostalgia. That comes as no surprise. After all, as Don Draper well knew, nostalgia sells things. For us to lean toward the future in this season, with the help of the likes of Isaiah, is a truly countercultural act.

Isaiah and the other prophets, and Jesus himself, declare that time is going somewhere. Time is not an endless circle, as the nature religions — so prevalent in their time — affirmed. The essence of time is not endless repetition of a cycle. Contrary to what Joni Mitchell affirmed in her song "The Circle Game," we are not "captive on the carousel of time." Rather, time is leading us somewhere.

Isaiah wants to make sure we understand that we are not being led back in time to some ideal past that is now gone. Ultimately, nostalgia can be dangerous to the life of faith because time doesn't lean backward toward the good old days. Time leans forward to something we have yet to experience. There is a story told through time, and we have not heard it all before, and we have yet to reach the full climax of that story, the climax that Isaiah's prophecy anticipates in the coming of the Messiah and the Peaceable Kingdom he brings. So God beckons us not to the past, but to the future, God's future. So where are you being tugged and where do you lean at such a time? Are you tugged by memories and leaning toward the past? If you are, that's understandable. I think we all are in one way or another. Nostalgia is a particular temptation at this time of year, in this season in which we are acutely aware of the passage of time. But how about this: Let's not stay there. With part of our beings, and with the help of the likes of Isaiah, and Jesus himself, let's lean forward in anticipation of what we have not yet seen and can only begin to imagine. The good old days, as good as they were, or as good as we may remember them to be, are nothing compared to what God has in store for us.

GIVE THANKS IN ALL CIRCUMSTANCES

1 Thessalonians 5:12-22

N O ONE IS BORN THANKFUL. Thankfulness doesn't come naturally to us, and sometimes it doesn't come at all. Rather, thankfulness is a quality that must be fostered and nurtured. But how? How do we teach our children to be thankful, and how do we lead ourselves in the ways of thankfulness? That question, though seemingly simple, is not easily answered.

We are enjoined in a variety of ways to count our blessings. Survey all that you have. Take stock of all you have been given. There is value in that, to be sure, but such an exercise does not in itself prompt thankfulness, because thankfulness has no direct correlation to abundance. If there were such a correlation, if we were given some abundance, we would be somewhat thankful, and if we were given more abundance, we would be more thankful. But it doesn't work that way, does it?

There is no direct correlation between thankfulness and abundance. In fact, here is an irony I confront anew every Thanksgiving holiday: the more we have, the less likely we are to thank God. Continuous bounty doesn't always create thankfulness; indeed, sometimes it actually seems to stamp out thankfulness.

We live in a time of extraordinary abundance, but that hasn't led us to greater thankfulness. In fact, it seems to me that another defining characteristic of our age is that we live with an extraordinary sense of entitlement. In other words, we have much, and for the most part it seems that we have concluded that we deserve all that we have and probably more.

Let me put it another way: Who is tempted to claim that he is a self-made man or she is a self-made woman? Is it the person who has few of the world's goods and has known little of earthly success? More likely it will be the person who has been given much, owns much.

I once heard of a man who consistently boasted that he was a self-made man until an exasperated friend finally declared, "Well, sir, that relieves the Lord of a terrific responsibility."

Obviously, such an attitude may relieve the Lord of responsibility, but it also deprives the Lord of thanks. True thanksgiving begins with humility, the humility to recognize that we did not create ourselves, that everything we are and everything we have is a gift.

The cartoon character Bart Simpson, when asked to offer thanks at a family meal, said, "Dear God, we bought all of this stuff with our own money, so thanks for nothing."

Bart Simpson's prayer summarizes all too well the reigning sentiments of our age. And often the more we have, the more likely we are to say, "Thanks for nothing." After all, the implications of thanksgiving are greater when we have much. The stakes are that much higher. There is more to protect. Those of us who have much and desire more feel the need to isolate ourselves from the realization that ultimately we really own nothing, that everything is from God and is God's. And so, those of us who have substantial abundance fence in our accumulated goods with self-assurances that everything we have is earned or deserved.

No, abundance doesn't necessarily lead to thankfulness. The very magnitude of what we have can numb us. When Alanna, our first child, was still very young, I remember learning to my surprise that a toy store is not a garden of delights for a young child. Not understanding money, she assumed that she could have anything she wanted. So in a toy store she bounced about like a ball in a pinball machine, wanting this and that so frantically that she didn't pause long enough to want anything very much at all. In a toy store there can be so many toys that a child can't begin to appreciate any one toy. In the end it can be much more pleasant to cuddle up with that single treasured teddy bear.

We adults can be similarly numbed when we're bombarded by bounty. Give a person one square meal a day, and he or she will find time and reason to give thanks. But give a person an opulent feast every night, and it won't be long before he or she begins to quibble over whether the meal really deserves that three-star rating. Isn't this the way with us? We can have so many blessings that we fail to note any of them.

And so, the Apostle Paul's urging to "Give thanks in all circumstances" is a reminder not just to those who are experiencing hardship, where blessings are so few. Those same words are also a reminder to us, who live amid bounty, where the blessings are so easily taken for granted. We need the reminder no less than others, and in many ways we need the reminder more. "Give thanks in all circumstances" when we seem to have so little and, yes, even when we obviously have so much.

Here I think Paul gives us the beginning of a response to our original question: How is thankfulness engendered? By "giving thanks in all circumstances," by continually offering thanks. The Psalmist enjoins — indeed, commands — the people to give thanks: "O give thanks to the LORD, for he is good, for his steadfast love endures forever. O give thanks to the God of gods, for his steadfast love endures forever. O give thanks to the Lord of lords, for his steadfast love endures forever" (Ps. 136:1-3). Notice that the Psalmist doesn't tell us to be thankful, but instead enjoins us to offer thanks. Offer thanks. Bless God's name. You may not feel like doing it. But do it anyway.

Jesus said, "Where your treasure is, there your heart will be also." We might be very familiar with this pronouncement, but if we don't read it with care, we might reverse the statement through a kind of scriptural dyslexia. We might read it to say, "Where your heart is, there will your treasure be also." That would make sense to us, because much of the time our dollars follow our heart's lead. We give to what matters to us. But that isn't what Jesus said.

That's the appeal we hear over and over again from, say, National Public Radio or our alma mater: If you care about this institution, you will write a check. In other words, "Where your heart is, there will your treasure be also." But Jesus didn't say that.

Jesus is speaking of a different dynamic: Give and spend where you want your heart to be, and then let your heart catch up. Don't just give to those things you care about. Give to the things you want to care about. Ask yourself, "If I were the sort of person I long to be, then what would I do? How would I spend my money?" Then do what you would do if you were that sort of person. Put your treasure where you want your heart to be. And if you do, says Jesus, your heart will go there. If you want to care more about the kind of car you drive, buy an expensive one. If you want to care more about property values, remodel your house. But if you want to grow in your faith, bring an offering to God. Wherever your treasure is, your heart is sure to follow.

Here, as elsewhere in the scriptural tradition, we are not told to feel a certain way; rather, we are enjoined to act in a certain manner. After all, feelings, unlike actions, cannot be governed by simple will. For instance, Jesus doesn't ask us to *feel* charitable toward our neighbors and our enemies. That would be asking something that isn't within our control. We simply cannot feel on command. Jesus is wise enough not to ask that of us. Instead, he asks us to act, to *act* charitably. Turn your cheek. Give to those who beg from you. Pray for your enemies. Give thanks to God. Don't wait until you feel like it. Nike could have borrowed their motto from Jesus: "Just do it."

It is here that we come upon another irony: it is by continually expressing thanks that we can come to be thankful. Day in and day out, in and out of season, offer thanks, perhaps at first just to get the feel of it and then, only in time, because you feel it. So sometimes, especially at first, we don't come to worship to offer our thanks to God because we are thankful. Rather, we come to worship to offer our thanks to God so that we might someday be thankful. Sometimes words of thanks need to be on our lips before, by some slow and largely imperceptible process, they can take up residence in our hearts.

I think, in our own simple way, we have some understanding of this. We say to our children — who, like their parents, were not born thankful — "Say 'thank you' to the gentleman." "What do you say to the nice lady?" We continually prompt, coax, urge, *demand* that thanks be offered. Do we put our children, and ourselves, through all of that just so they will behave in a polite manner? Perhaps. But I think we do this also because we have some understanding that continually offering thanks, day in and day out, in and out of season, whether we feel like it or not, eventually helps engender a spirit of thankfulness.

It may not begin as an easy flow of grace and gratitude. It may begin slowly, because we're so accustomed to receiving God's gifts with callused hands. So we begin by saying thanks, not just one day a year, but by practicing thanksgiving every day and seeking opportunities to do so in every circumstance.

In an intriguing little book called *365 Thank Yous,* John Kralik writes about his experience of writing a thank-you note a day for an entire year. He didn't resolve to write all of those thank-you notes at a time when he was feeling particularly grateful. In fact, it was at a particularly low time in his life. His small law firm was losing money and losing its lease. He was going through a difficult divorce. He lived in a small, stuffy apartment where he often slept on the floor under an ancient air conditioner. He was middle-aged, overweight, and at the end of his rope.

Then, one day, on a hike on a mountain trail, he literally got lost and didn't know how to get home. By the time he found his way and made it down the mountain, he had a plan. He would write a thank-you note each day for a year. But even as he made that resolution, he had his doubts. He writes, "My only problem [was]: Did I have anything to be grateful for? The way my life was going, I hardly thought so."[1]

Kralik got started anyway, beginning by writing notes to the people close to him, his family and friends. But then it got harder. "One day," he writes, "I just couldn't think of anybody to thank." But on his way to work, he stopped at his regular Starbucks, where the barista greeted him by name — "John, your usual *venti?*" — and with a big smile. Kralik reflected, "I thought, this is really kind of a great gift in this day and age of impersonal relationships, that someone had cared enough to learn my name and what I drank in the morning."[2] So he wrote the barista a thank-you note. And so it went through the year. Each day a thank-you note, each day a day of thanksgiving.

1. John Kralik, *365 Thank Yous* (New York: Hyperion, 2010), p. 17.
2. Kralik, *365 Thank Yous,* p. 81.

The most interesting part of the book is Kralik's reflections on how the experience of expressing thanks day in and day out changed the way he approached life. It even got him to church. He writes:

> I had considered myself something of an atheist for years, but I started going to this church [near the end of that year]. The music was plentiful, delivered with . . . genuine enthusiasm. The dominant message was that grace was still available. To everyone. Even to me. I can deal with that, I thought. Through the process of writing thank-you notes, I had developed a notion of being blessed with grace. . . .[3]

Yes, there is something about offering thanks that makes us whole. There is something about offering thanks that can make us feel, with Kralik, that we are "blessed with grace."

In fact, in the New Testament, the word that is translated as "thanks" is the very same word that is sometimes translated as "grace." The word in Greek, *charis*, or "grace," may define an act of giving or an act of receiving: if giving, the word means "gift or unearned favor"; if receiving, then the word is best translated as "gratitude." We see a reflection of this double meaning in the prayers that are offered before a meal. Some families "say grace," while others, "give thanks." It is the same word *(charis)* in both instances.

I like to think of it as the endless echo of grace. We receive a gift in the same spirit in which it is given — it is all grace. We can even lose track of where it begins and where it ends, for it all seems to be of one piece.

People whose lives are not traced with gratitude — whose lives are governed by a sense of entitlement or grievance — are miserable. No matter how much they have — in material

---

3. Kralik, *365 Thank Yous*, p. 178.

wealth, health, success — if it is not accompanied by a sense of gratitude, their lives are fractured or incomplete. They are not made whole.

By contrast, those whose lives are marked with gratitude, infused with thankfulness, join in the echo of grace and receive a particular blessing reserved for them. They are made well. They are made whole.

Beloved Christian author C. S. Lewis observed that grateful people are emotionally healthy people. "Praise," he said, "almost seems to be inner health made audible." I'm quite sure Lewis would accept this friendly amendment to his observation: Words of thanksgiving are also something like inner health made audible.

CHRISTMAS GIFTS

Luke 2:1-20

I N OUR HOUSEHOLD, DURING THE LEAD-UP to Christmas, we receive many unsolicited catalogs in the mail from a variety of retailers. I don't know how they get our address, and I don't know how to get off their mailing lists, so that time of year our mailbox overflows like the pail of water from *The Sorcerer's Apprentice* — always more and more, a torrent of catalogs.

One night I flipped through a handful of them. Here are just a few of the many gifts being offered at Christmas.

There is "The Remote-Controlled Rolling Beverage Cooler." If someone across the room looks thirsty, you don't have to get out of your seat to serve them. You can use the remote control to send the cooler in their direction.

There is "The Complete Swiss Army Knife," which is like the more conventional Swiss Army knives, but it includes 87 tools all in a row. In addition to knives, screwdrivers, and the like, it boasts other gadgets, including a 20-gauge shotgun choke-tube tool (whatever that is), a laser pointer, and a toothpick. Those of you who are golfers might want to know that the knife includes three golf tools (club face cleaner, shoe spike wrench, and divot repair tool). It's quite comprehensive. And it should be. It costs $1,400.

Or how about the case for wristwatches? It automatically winds up to four watches at a time so you don't have to. In the "You'll Shoot Your Eye Out" category, there's the Double-Barreled Marshmallow Crossbow, which shoots 25 mini-marshmallows from each barrel. In case you can't imagine how you would use such a thing, the catalog suggests that it's "suitable as an offensive weapon for assaulting a sibling's doll house." Merry Christmas.

Then there's the toaster that can emblazon the emblem of your favorite team on your morning toast. When I told a friend about this, he informed me that there's a toaster that can do the same thing with the image of Jesus. I thought that was just too strange to be true until I found a Web site dedicated to Jesus toasters. True story. All of my stories are true — and some I wish were not.

Or there's the alarm clock for the sleepyhead who has a hard time getting out of bed in the morning. It has no snooze button, and it can't be turned off until the user solves a mathematical equation. Presumably, by that time he or she is too wide awake to go back to sleep.

Another nominee in the category of things nobody needs is "The Full Bottle Wine Glass," a beautifully proportioned wineglass from Italy that can hold a full bottle of wine.

To spend an evening with these catalogs is to be so awash in a consumer culture gone wild that you almost feel like you have to take a shower afterwards. You go from saying to yourself, "I don't need this stuff" to saying, "Nobody needs this stuff."

Do not assume, however, that I'm a fan of practical gifts. No, my position on that has been clear since I was a boy. I know that everyone needs socks. But not wrapped up and under the Christmas tree. (I apologize to anyone who has already bought socks for a loved one, and offer an extra apology to anyone who has already wrapped them and put them under the tree.)

In Dylan Thomas's beloved short story "A Child's Christmas in Wales," he tells a small boy about the Christmas celebrations of his youth. The boy eagerly prompts him: "And then the presents?" Thomas replies, "There were the Useful Presents: engulfing mufflers of the old coach days and mittens made for giant sloths; zebra scarfs that could be tug-o-warred down to the galoshes. . . ." And he goes on from there until the boy can't stand it any longer and interrupts, "Go on to the Useless Presents." (I am that boy.)

And then Thomas goes on to catalog all the Useless Presents that delighted him when he was a boy. Nothing elaborate or expensive. His family didn't have much money. But these presents were impractical, useless for anything except delight — the candies and other sweet treats, the little toys and games, the packet of candy cigarettes. Ah, yes. "You put one in your mouth," he recalls, "and you stood at the corner of the street and you waited for hours, in vain, for an old lady to scold you for smoking a cigarette, and then with a smirk you ate it." Thomas obviously thought that a perfect gift. Useless. Delightful.

We all know the song "The Twelve Days of Christmas":

On the first day of Christmas
My true love gave to me
A partridge in a pear tree. . . .

And the song's not over until we have two turtle doves, three French hens, and all those swans swimming, drummers drumming, jumpers jumping, cows a-leaping (or whatever — I can never keep them all straight). Everyone loves that song — and it is a celebration of completely inappropriate and largely useless gifts. A partridge in a pear tree? Not a practical gift. But that's the beauty of it. That's what makes it worth singing about. Who would want to sing a song about the gift of a new frying pan?

The late Halford Luccock, who a generation ago taught at Yale Divinity School, thought we should take our cue from the song: "Give your true love an inappropriate gift. Don't get grandma another lace cap or pair of woolen mittens. She has plenty already, and besides she hates the things. Get her a little bottle of Chanel No. 5 or a set of lipsticks or a pair of dancing slippers."

"And for father — lay off the neckties and the conservative scarf. Get him a Lionel electric train, appropriate for age nine. (All his own; children, keep away!) Dad has always had a yen for one."

Then Luccock reflects: "The best gifts of love are those which show a lovely lack of common sense. They are not practical. Flowers (they fade, don't they?), a bracelet (always a nuisance). It is usually on the twenty-fifth anniversary that a husband gives a vacuum cleaner."[1]

Wait . . . a vacuum cleaner for a twenty-fifth anniversary gift? What husband would do that? Well, I did, actually — but it wasn't our twenty-fifth anniversary. It was Karen's fiftieth birthday. But she made me do it. She made it clear that it was her heart's desire. Truly. And now I see why. When she glides around the house with that vacuum cleaner, she looks as happy as Ginger Rogers dancing with Fred Astaire. From that I learned that some useful presents can have a bit of delight in them.

Anyway, I digress. . . .

In the end, I think Halford Luccock was right: The best gifts do not exhibit common sense. They are impractical.

He concludes: "There is high precedent for all this. The first Christmas gift was highly inappropriate — a baby in a barn. Who wanted that? No one clapped and said, 'Goody, goody,

---

1. Halford E. Luccock, *A Sprig of Holly* (New York: Pilgrim Press, 1978), pp. 9-10.

just what I wanted!' That is, no one except a few souls who could really see — some shepherds, his mother."[2]

So, although I refuse to celebrate the orgy of conspicuous consumption, I do delight in the taste of grace. You see, grace is something we cannot deserve, do not really ask for, a delightful something extra. And sometimes it is only in receiving it that we realize it is what we wanted all along.

One of the best Christmas gifts I ever received was from my brother. He's ten years older than I am, and I was twelve at the time. He gave me a bright red ascot. (For the sartorially limited: An ascot is a kind of fancy scarf, usually made of silk, which you tie around your neck and tuck into your shirt. Very dashing.) I didn't ask for an ascot. I didn't know I *could* ask for such a thing. I immediately loved it. I loved it because my big brother gave it to me, because my best friend, Drew Hart, didn't have anything like it, and because . . . well, because it was a bright red ascot. And that was long before I learned that the French sometimes translate one of Jesus' Beatitudes as "Blessed are the *debonair*, for they shall inherit the earth."

Just to be clear, when I was twelve I didn't like receiving clothes for Christmas. But an ascot isn't an article of clothing. A necktie might be considered clothing, but an ascot is an event, that something extra, that delightful little grace note, that taste of grace. I never would have asked for it. In fact, it was only in receiving it that I realized that it was what I wanted all along. And that's why it has always seemed to me to be the perfect Christmas gift.

When I was a child, my parents showered me with gifts — not only gifts at Christmas, but throughout the year; not just gifts of toys and Christmas treats, but gifts of life and love. They didn't give me these gifts because I deserved them. They knew who was naughty and nice — but it didn't seem

2. Luccock, A *Sprig of Holly*, p. 10.

to matter. And, indeed, there was nothing I could give in return, even if they had been looking for anything in return. But there was something in me that longed to be the giver of gifts instead of always being the receiver of gifts. So one year I wrapped the plaster-of-Paris hand-print paperweight I made in school and put it under the tree. I suppose it wasn't the first gift I gave my parents, but I remember the sense of anticipation I felt at being able to give this gift.

I have no reason to believe that my parents were eager to receive a hand-print paperweight. To my knowledge, it never appeared on any of their gift lists. And now I can see that they didn't need it. It wasn't one of Dylan Thomas's "Useful Presents." But when they opened the package, it was with "oohs" and "ahs." They thanked me and embraced me. They didn't need to receive such a gift, but I think they probably saw that I needed to give it. And when my mother died, among the things my siblings and I discovered in her apartment, carefully wrapped in tissue paper and safely laid in a drawer, was that hand-print paperweight. The gracious givers of everything I had and everything I am became, for my sake, the gracious receivers of my gift to them.

I think God does the same for us. God needs nothing from us. Indeed, everything we are and everything we have, including the great gift we celebrate in this season, we have received from God's hand. We cannot give anything in return. But God also sees that we feel a need to respond, and God allows us to do just that by receiving our gifts of praise and devotion — useless presents, but delightful ones. And the God who has given us everything, grace upon grace, graciously receives those gifts.

HOW TO THROW A PARTY

Luke 14:12-24

I F YOU WANT TO LEARN HOW to throw a party, there are resources that can help. Just read a book by one of the author-
ities on the subject. The venerable twin towers of respect-
ability, Emily Post and Amy Vanderbilt, both wrote some sage
advice, and for those who want a more contemporary take,
Judith Martin (who writes under the name "Miss Manners")
offers good suggestions, as does Jacqueline Whitmore.

Without getting into the fine points, like whether the
wine glass goes to the right or the left of the water glass, here
are some of the basic principles.

First, the proper party begins with a carefully constructed
guest list. The key is to invite people with whom you have
much in common — that is, family members, friends, and
business associates. It is also permissible to include those who
have invited you to their home several times whom you feel
you simply must repay before it gets too embarrassing. Then
there are those who have never invited you to their homes,
and you wonder why, because you've entertained them many
times, and besides, anyone who's anyone seems to get invited
to their parties. So you'll try again this time in the hope that
they'll be so impressed or so whatever-it-takes that they'll
finally issue you an invitation in return. There are the people

you want to know better, the important people, the right people. Obviously, they also belong on the guest list. Above all, all the guests should be from the same thin social stratum, live on the same side of the tracks. Your party isn't a time to show anyone how the other half lives.

Next, the invitations. They must be clear and gracious. They should state what kind of party it is, what time the guests are expected to arrive, and, of course, what kind of attire would be appropriate. It's best to be very specific on this last point to avoid embarrassment. A friend of my parents used to send engraved invitations that stated quite simply "Black tie or white tie," and then, in parentheses, "Dr. Jenkins will be wearing white tie," just to save guests the embarrassment of arriving at a formal occasion in a mere tuxedo when the host will be wearing tails. And, of course, it's appropriate to request a response to the invitation.

When the responses are received, it's important to study the guest list carefully in order to plan the seating arrangements. Here the key is to put people together who have much in common and who will feel at ease with one another. For instance, it's best not to put together people who, in the past, have had unpleasant business dealings with one another, or, for that matter, to put a Republican next to a Democrat. (Independents always come in handy as a kind of buffer.) People who don't get along belong at opposite ends of the table, where they can do no more than exchange chilly smiles. And, as the host, you can make sure that the important people, the right people, are seated next to you.

If you follow these simple principles, you're well on your way to throwing a successful party, a party that is proper, pleasant, and comfortable.

But this isn't the end of the matter, because there's another source that tells us how to throw a party. The source is older than Miss Manners, older even than Emily Post and

Amy Vanderbilt. It is the Bible, and the expert quoted there is Jesus.

Jesus offered his guidance on how to throw a party while he was attending a party himself at the home of one of the important people, one of the right people, a ruler. Around the table were influential priests and successful lawyers and other people of note. In short, it was the kind of party that would do a first-century Emily Post proud, the kind of party that surely would be mentioned in the social pages of the local paper.

It was in the midst of this gathering, as they were beginning to pass around the kosher foie gras, that Jesus said, "When you give a dinner or a banquet, do not invite your friends or your brothers or your kinsmen or your rich neighbors, lest they also invite you in return, and you be repaid. But when you give a feast, invite the poor, the maimed, the lame, and the blind, and you will be blessed, because they cannot repay you. You will be repaid at the resurrection of the just." Someone obviously forgot to tell Jesus that a proper guest at such a proper party doesn't say anything nearly as challenging as this.

But then Jesus went on to tell a parable that only made matters worse. It was a parable about the ultimate party, the feast of the Kingdom of God. And through the parable, Jesus made clear that the people who would miss that party were some of the same people who were seated around the table with him. It's not that they wouldn't be invited. To be sure, they would receive the same invitation as everyone else, but they would all find one reason or another why they couldn't come. So, instead, the people who would be seated in the places of honor, next to the Divine Host, would be all the people who never would be found around a ruler's table, the poor and maimed and blind and lame, people who were distinguished by nothing but their obvious need and by a willingness to accept the invitation.

When God is throwing the party, the protocol isn't anything that Emily Post would recognize. When God is throwing the party, there is no thought given to inviting only those who can repay the favor, because who can repay God? When God is throwing the party, people are invited who have nothing in common except the only thing that matters: they have all accepted the invitation.

When God is throwing the party, the invitations are issued without a hint about proper attire because it's a come-as-you-are party, as all of God's parties are, which is another way of saying that God's parties are be-who-you-are parties. You don't have to try to look like everyone else or like everyone expects you to look — respectable, buoyant, and put-together. You can come to this party as someone whose very life is unpolished and torn.

When God is throwing the party, you never know who will be there or who will sit next to you. The mutual-fund manager is seated next to the panhandler she always passes on her way to work. The store owner is next to the person he just fired, and a doctor is next to the woman who just sued him for malpractice. Rush Limbaugh may be sitting beside a single mother on welfare. Antonin Scalia may have to strike up a conversation with a gay rights activist. Yes, all the "right" people will be there — that is, everyone who accepted the Lord's invitation. And seated next to the host at the places of honor are not the dignitaries, the celebrities, the distinguished people of position and prominence, but rather the poor, the hurting, the outcast, people who have distinguished themselves only by their need.

Jesus says that this is what the Kingdom of God will be like. It will be a feast unlike any other party we are likely to attend — in this social season or any other. And although we don't know just when that party will take place, every time we gather as a church, we're invited to a kind of warm-up for that occasion. After all, the church is the place where God throws parties, and any party where God is host will reflect elements of that ultimate party that is still to come.

For nine years I served a church located in the downtown area of Burlington, Vermont. We were aware that many in our church were alone for Thanksgiving, so one year we invited church members to come to a Thanksgiving Day dinner at the church. We didn't take reservations. We didn't charge any money. We didn't plan the menu. We simply asked people to bring some Thanksgiving dish to contribute to the feast.

When the day came, the people all pitched in like members of a large extended family to put the meal on the table. We had more turkeys and cranberry relish and candied yams and pumpkin pie than we could possibly eat. And because there are those of us who think that the leftovers are the best part of Thanksgiving dinner, we sent everyone home with some. And we still had plenty to send over to the homeless shelter.

The next year someone suggested that we invite the folks from the homeless shelter to join us for the Thanksgiving Day meal at the church. Some felt that this would be a disservice to the homeless poor, who would feel uncomfortable coming to a church and sitting with a bunch of middle-class folks for such a meal; they suggested that we again take meals to the shelter instead. In the end, we decided to invite the residents of the shelter to join us at the church. We sent out invitations to the shelter and posted a few notices around town. Fewer of our own church members showed up that year, although of course they were invited, perhaps because they were the ones who felt uncomfortable about sharing Thanksgiving with such a motley collection of people.

But every seat was filled. College students, unable to get home for the holidays, showed up. The residents of the shelter came in great numbers. There were church members, some of whom were alone and others who brought their families. People who were dressed in special holiday clothes sat next to others who, because they lived on the streets, hadn't changed their clothes in days, if not weeks. In other words, all the right people were there, all the people who accepted the invitation, and there was a place for everyone.

During the meal the social hall buzzed with conversation. I saw one distinguished doctor making a valiant attempt to engage in small talk with a homeless man. After all, how can you begin a conversation when you can't ask about a person's job, and when you don't want to mention the weather because it's cold outside, and when the meal is over, one of you will be returning to the streets? One young college student, stranded in town for the holidays, was asked to carve a turkey, something he probably never would have been asked to do if he had been at home. A woman who lived alone assumed the role of hostess at her table. One resident of the shelter, whom I recognized as the one who regularly picked soda cans out of the trash for the cash he could get for them at the supermarket, led us all in a rousing rendition of "Now Thank We All Our God."

A woman who had been working in the kitchen since early morning finally emerged and stood next to me by the coffee urn. We surveyed this teeming, joyous, chaotic, vivacious scene, and she said, in astonishment, "It's just like Jesus' parable of the feast."

Exactly. It was the right event, with all the right people, held in its rightful home — because, you see, the church is the place where we get to enjoy the warm-up for the feast of the Kingdom of God. The church is the place where God loves to throw parties. And this is the kind of party God has in mind.

ARE YOU TALKING TO ME?

Matthew 10:24-33

THERE ARE TWO KINDS OF JESUS' TEACHINGS I find difficult to hear, two categories of Jesus' teachings that
convict me to such an extent that I have to resist the
temptation to cover my ears and sing a loud song. There are
those teachings that clearly are directed to me, and there are
those teachings that clearly are *not* directed to me.

The first category — those teachings that clearly are directed to me — includes, among other passages, the entire
Sermon on the Mount. The most pointed words in that sermon find the bull's-eye in my heart:

> "You have heard that it was said to those of old, 'You shall
> not kill; and whoever kills shall be liable to judgment.' But
> I say to you that every one who is angry with his brother or
> sister shall be liable to judgment." (Matt. 5:21)
> "Beware of practicing your piety before others." (6:1)
> "Do not lay up for yourselves treasures on earth, where
> moth and rust consume and where thieves break in and
> steal, but lay up for yourselves treasures in heaven." (6:19)
> "Do not be anxious about tomorrow, for tomorrow will
> be anxious for itself." (6:34)
> "Judge not, that you be not judged." (7:1)

"Why do you see the speck that is in your brother's eye
but do not notice the log that is in your own eye?" (7:3)

I could go on, of course, but I'd rather not. All of those
teachings are just too clearly directed to me. When Jesus gets
going like that, I feel like the man who reported that he felt
so convicted by John Wesley's preaching that he would bury
his face in his hands. When he raised his head, he expected
to find the entire congregation staring at him because he was
convinced that the preacher was talking only to him.

The second category of Jesus' teachings that I find difficult
to hear includes those that so clearly are *not* directed to me.
In one such instance, Jesus is preparing his disciples to go out
to preach and teach in his name. In some sense, he's preparing
all of his followers. He's preparing us. He's telling us what we
need to know to be sent forth in his name, and from the beginning he makes it clear that his followers are going to have
a rough go of it. Jesus says, in essence, "As my followers, you
can't expect to be treated any better than I am. In fact, you'll
probably have it worse. They have called me Beelzebul. Imagine what worse things they will do to you" (Matt. 10:24-25).

When I read that, I think to myself, *Are you talking to me?
I don't think so.* I haven't been reviled or persecuted or cursed
for being a follower of Jesus — at least, not in ways that Jesus seems to have imagined I would be. After all, I attended
Yale Divinity School, and when I graduated, I went on to do
all of the things I was trained to do — to be a leader in the
church and in society — and, for the most part, I have been
appreciated for it. I've led a rather comfortable life. Neither
I nor the members of the churches I've served were reviled.
We were appreciated. The last church I served was the oldest
institution in town. It was set on a hill, on the most prominent intersection in town, as if presiding over all that could
be surveyed from that perch. And even people who never set

foot in the church building seemed to like the fact that it was there. Why else would they put a photo of the church's steeple on the cover of the local phone book? Obviously, we didn't pose much of a threat to anyone. So Jesus' words seem not to be addressed to us. We were not reviled or persecuted or cursed for being his followers.

Does that mean that we found ways to do our master one better, to proclaim the Realm of God in ways that everyone is ready to accept? Or, in the two thousand years since Jesus sent out the first wave of his followers with words of warning and encouragement, has the culture really come around? Perhaps society is so transformed that there's no one left to revile us.

But, alas, there's another possibility. Perhaps we're no longer worth persecuting. Perhaps we don't pose that kind of threat. Perhaps we no longer represent the kind of clear alternative to the ways of the surrounding culture. And that's why I feel convicted by this word, because clearly it isn't directed to me. It assumes that I, as a Christian, would pose a threat to earthly powers, that I would be worth persecuting.

I was once invited to participate in a meeting at a center for leadership in Washington, D.C. This center, associated with a prominent church, aims to equip people at the beginning of their careers to lead as Christians — not in the church but in the secular workplace. They are asking, "How does a Christian faithfully exercise leadership in the world?" When I asked what I might read in advance of that meeting, I was referred to several books, including *Jesus CEO* by Laurie Beth Jones. This popular book has about forty short chapters, each with an engaging title that conjures a characteristic of Jesus worth emulating. Here is a sampling:

He Kept in Constant Contact with His Boss

He Believed in Himself

He Said Thank You

He Formed a Team

He Said, "Why Not Me?"

And here's my personal favorite:

He Was a Turnaround Specialist[1]

But I couldn't help noticing that one chapter that's conspicuously missing is the one entitled "He Was Crucified." Have we done our master one better? Have we figured out how to proclaim the Realm of God without having to pay the consequences? Or perhaps we're simply not worth persecuting anymore. Those who run the leadership center clearly assume that whoever is supervising these young leaders in the workplace would love to have them get this kind of training in Christian leadership. It would make them better employees with more promising futures. But what if the program were evaluated by how many people went back to work and were reviled, perhaps for asking questions that no one else dared ask, or for insisting on a higher code of conduct than others were willing to adhere to, or for failing to see the bottom line as the sole measure of success? Would that be too much to expect from a Christian leadership center? Perhaps they could keep track of how many folks were demoted sometime after they left the program. After all, Jesus sent his followers off with words of encouragement, yes, but also with words of warning.

Søren Kierkegaard once mused, "I wonder if a man hand-

1. Laurie Beth Jones, *Jesus CEO: Using Ancient Wisdom for Visionary Leadership* (New York: Hachette, 1996).

ing another man an extremely sharp, polished, two-edged instrument would hand it over with the air, gestures, and expression of one delivering a bouquet of flowers? Would not this be madness? What does one do, then? Convinced of the excellence of the dangerous instrument, one recommends it unreservedly, to be sure, but in such a way that in a certain sense one warns against it. So it is with Christianity. . . ."[2] Indeed, when Jesus handed over the gospel to his followers, he did so with a warning: "They have called me Beelzebul. Imagine what they are going to call you." But did we need that warning? Was he talking to us?

During the Clinton administration, at the height of the debate over whether gay folks should be allowed to serve in the military, Duke ethicist Stanley Hauerwas wrote an op-ed piece in the *Charlotte Observer* called "Why Gays (as a Group) Are Morally Superior to Christians (as a Group)."[3] In that article he observes that the military is somehow threatened by having gay soldiers, but they're fine with having Christian soldiers. And he tries to imagine what it would be like if Christians took their own discipleship so seriously that they would pose a threat, that they would be so dangerous to have around that the military would exclude them as a group. For example, Christians are potentially dangerous for morale in the barracks. You don't want these people gathering at night holding hands with heads bowed. Who knows what kind of disgusting behavior they might be engaged in? Why, they might be praying for the enemy! Could you trust someone who would think it more important to die than to kill unjustly? When they eat as part of their worship, they say be-

2. Quoted in *Parables of Kierkegaard*, ed. Thomas C. Oden (Princeton: Princeton University Press, 1978).

3. Stanley Hauerwas, "Why Gays (as a Group) Are Morally Superior to Christians (as a Group)," in *The Hauerwas Reader* (Durham, N.C.: Duke University Press, 2001), pp. 519-21.

lievers cannot come to the meal with blood on their hands. And would you want to shower with such people? They might try to baptize you. And that, concludes Hauerwas, is why gays as a group are morally superior to Christians as a group — because Christians as a group don't do those things that would exclude them from being in the military. In that setting, we are not reviled, persecuted, or cursed. In fact, it's hard to find a setting in which we are.

And yet . . .

And yet, Jesus still knows how to get his friends into trouble.

I'm thinking of the star high-school lacrosse player who misses a week of practice during spring vacation because he's with his church, building homes in partnership with the poor through Habitat for Humanity. He knows that he'll have to sit out two games when he gets back — it's the usual punishment for missing practice — but when the team loses both games, the coach is quoted in the school paper as saying that they lost those games because this young man didn't play. The coach did everything but call him Beelzebul.

I'm also thinking of the woman who lives in the neighborhood where her church is establishing a home for adults with developmental disabilities. The whole neighborhood has been up in arms — property values, you know. So she invites all her neighbors to a reception at the new home and asks the young adults who are now living there to pass the hors d'oeuvres.

Then there's the person who left a prestigious professional position to do something that more directly serves people in need. We might call it "an alternative career path." She calls it "following Jesus." Less money, of course. She knew that going in. But fewer friends, too, because she doesn't quite fit in her usual circles in the same way she did before.

Or how about the fourteen-year-old boy who calls his parents from summer camp. "How are things going?" the parents ask. "All right, I guess. I gave the vespers meditation last night before lights out. I told my cabin that I don't think it's right for someone to be called 'gay' as a put-down, that there's nothing wrong with being gay." The parents ask, "How'd they take it?" A long pause. "They didn't get it. No one really understood what I was trying to say." "And what gave you the idea to use that as the subject of your meditation?" "I guess I have you to blame," the boy says with a bit of a laugh. "You and the church."

Then there's the young personal financial advisor, with a wife and three young children at home, who's getting pressure from his supervisor to push certain financial products, even though those products aren't suitable for many of his customers. He's supposed to act like he's giving impartial advice and at the same time recommend only those products from which the firm derives the greatest profit. He can't be fired for refusing to go along with the scheme. But there are ways in which his life can be — and is — made difficult. So he quits.

And there's the attorney who sixteen years ago agreed to defend someone on death row on a pro-bono basis. Sixteen years of arguments, motions, and appeals. For most of those years, this lawyer is the only contact his client has with the outside world. So, in addition to his official correspondence, the attorney writes his client chatty letters. He sends him pencils and chewing gum. When the final appeal is denied, he gets on a plane and flies to Alabama with his thirty-five-year-old son so that someone other than the guards and state officials will be there when his client is executed. And when he approaches the prison, there are demonstrators outside holding signs that commend both the condemned prisoner and his lawyer to the fires of hell.

Yes, Jesus still knows how to get his friends into trouble. All of those people are members of one congregation I served, all ordinary people in some way aiming to be followers of Jesus and getting themselves into trouble in the process.

None of those folks are exactly reviled or persecuted. They aren't undertaking heroic deeds on a grand scale. Certainly they don't represent the magnitude of all we're called to be as followers of Jesus. No, these are just small incidents, little incursions and inroads, small glimpses, cracks in the established order through which a light shines. Just that. Something small.

In the same passage in which Jesus warns his followers that they will be reviled and persecuted, he also says that God watches over small things with great care — like sparrows, the smallest of all birds. Jesus reminds us that God likes to work with small things — things like mustard seeds and pinches of salt and teaspoons of yeast. And sparrows.

When Jesus gives his followers these instructions, it is with soaring words and high expectations, as if he's asking them — asking us — to mount up with the wings of an eagle. In response, I want to ask, "Are you talking to me?"

But then Jesus adds, "And God watches over the sparrows." And then I know he is talking to me, after all.

REVELATION IN
RETROSPECT

Luke 24:13-32

I T ISN'T A LONG TRIP, BY MOST STANDARDS — just about seven miles from Jerusalem to their destination in Emmaus. But for these two followers of Jesus, it's probably one of the longest hikes imaginable. After all, their master and teacher is now dead, and he dragged all their dreams into death with him. As they walk, they're joined by a stranger who asks, "What are you folks talking about?" They stop right in their tracks and pounce on the stranger (not because the question is all that bad, but probably because they need to pounce on someone): "Haven't you heard? Have you been living under a rock or something? It's all about the man Jesus. He had done some incredible things, held out a promise to us and to all people — and they killed him. And all our hopes and dreams with him. Now we're getting some stories from a group of women that he's actually raised from the dead. They're tormenting us with stories about an empty tomb, and it's a bit much to take."

Then, for some reason, the stranger launches into a Bible lesson, proving just how out of touch he really is. He jumps right into it, explaining about how the prophets had predicted this would happen, how the Messiah had to suffer these things before entering into his glory. If nothing else, that stranger helps them pass the time and helps take their minds off their present troubles. So when they reach their destination, they invite the stranger to eat with them because it's getting late. The stranger seems glad to accept.

When they sit down to eat, the stranger takes some bread, blesses it, breaks it, and begins to pass it around. Something in that moment — is it the words he speaks or the way the bread crumbles when he breaks it? — opens the disciples' eyes. They see clearly. It comes to them. They remember other times when he had broken bread with them. In that moment the stranger Jesus vanishes, and they remember something else: "Didn't our hearts burn when he explained the Scriptures to us on the road?" The strange and important thing to note about that comment is that in the account we are given no clue — perhaps they had no clue — that their hearts were anything but stone cold. It's only in looking back that they say their hearts burned.

Which is right? Are they remembering falsely? Revising the past so that they can live with themselves in the present? Is this fanciful nostalgia? Or is it clear understanding at last?

It has become commonplace to observe that we sometimes have a way of revising the past to serve our own purposes. When we look back on the past, our memory plays tricks on us, makes it seem better than it was. Nostalgia can seem like nothing more than a longing to get back to a time that never was. We look on the past with what we call "rose-colored glasses." And as we become misty-eyed, we take the sharp edge off what were a lot of hurts and disappointments.

By comparison, the present seems drab and decidedly more cruel. But then, we live in the present and can see it more clearly. At least, such is the assumption; often this may be the case. There is another possibility, however.

Sometimes, perhaps even often, we can see the past more clearly than we see the present. The present we have once, but the past we can go back to. What we call "rose-colored glasses" may actually improve our vision. We're too limited to fully appreciate things as they go by. We need more time. It's as if we go back into the past again and again to finish the job of appreciation we couldn't complete the first time around.

For instance, when a person dies or moves away, suddenly people have good things to say about him or her. Are they wrong? In many cases, probably not. When that person was with you, his faults, the petty things that used to bug you about him — they got in the way. You couldn't see clearly. Now, as you look back, those things recede, and it's as if a veil has been lifted. You may continue to see the faults and flaws clearly enough, but what you see most of all is what a blessing it was to know this person.

Skeptics like to point out that much of the Bible was written about events that had long since passed at the time of the writing. For instance, the First Gospel was written about twenty years after Jesus' death. The skeptics raise this point to question the verity and reliability of Scripture. But I would suggest that in some ways the stories may reflect added understanding because they were written in retrospect. It is in looking back that we can see how God is at work in our lives. At the time we can be too close, too confused by the events that swirl around us.

When Moses led the exiled people of Israel across the Red Sea, I don't think that as they tromped through the mud they turned to each other and said, "See how God is leading us out of Egypt!" At the time, they probably said something more like, "By golly, what a lucky break!" It is only later, when they look back, that they see something else going on in their escape, that something else called God.

The same can be true in our personal histories as well: it is in looking back that we can understand. As the Danish theologian Søren Kierkegaard pointed out, the challenge we face is that we must live life forward, while only understanding it backward.

Reflecting on his own life, Frederick Buechner writes, "You get married, a child is born or not born, in the middle of the night there is a knocking at the door, on the way home through the park you see a man feeding pigeons, all the tests come in negative and the doctor gives you back your life again: incident follows incident helter-skelter leading apparently nowhere, but then once in a while there is the suggestion of purpose, meaning, direction, the suggestion of plot, the suggestion that, however clumsily, your life is trying to tell you something."[1]

Most often these kinds of insights come only in retrospect. It is in looking back that we can understand — not that everything turned out for the best (because seldom is that the case), but that somehow God was at work. In looking back we can see that our lives tell a story, that events came together, clustered in certain patterns to tell us something, and that something may be God. In looking back we can see God really was with us. God really was in that place all along, and we didn't know it. Our hearts really did burn. Those really were blessed times.

Why don't we just try to appreciate life as we live it? Why can't we appreciate people before they die or leave us? Ah, but it is difficult. Surely you've noticed that. Such sensitivity and perception usually elude us.

When our children were very young, we lived in Vermont, and we had just built a small sunroom onto the back of our house. It quickly became our favorite room. On a sunny day it was bright and warm. And when snow swirled outside, we felt as if we were in the midst of one of those small glass

1. Frederick Buechner, *The Alphabet of Grace* (New York: Harper & Row, 1970), p. 10.

domes that, when you shake it, depicts a winter scene complete with falling snow. We ate most of our meals in this room.

A meal with young children is always something of a circus, complete with ringmasters, clowns, wild animals, and a sometimes appreciative audience. During our family meals, feats of wonder were performed. Todd's favorite trick was throwing toast over his shoulder and never once having it land jelly-side up. Adult conversations were often left suspended in mid-air for minutes at a time. And who needs clown make-up when there's plenty of spaghetti sauce to go around? Some of those meals were accompanied by loud laughter, an appropriate response to a comedy of errors. But there were other times when it was hard to get into the spirit of things. I often longed for a meal at a quiet table in a corner, rather than under the big top.

Whoever invented winter must not have had young children. After one particularly long winter weekend, our family assembled for dinner in the sunroom. It included the usual spirited performances, but I wasn't amused. Not in the slightest. I was quick to volunteer to clear the table and get dessert, a precious opportunity for a moment of quiet. When I left, I closed the French doors that separated the sunroom from the rest of the house.

As I headed back I paused, not out of dread, but from something much more compelling. The room in which I stood was dark, but the sunroom was brightly lit. Through the French doors I could see my family. It was the same rowdy circus, but peering through the panes of the door I was no longer annoyed. Rather, I felt embraced by the scene. Out of sight and at some distance, I could savor the moment and remember and feel how much I loved this crazy bundle of people we called our family. But not every moment is such a moment. Most often such moments occur at a distance in time and space. That is, most often we see such things only in retrospect.

In Thornton Wilder's play *Our Town*, Emily, who had died at a young age, is given the opportunity to go back and live one day again. She chooses a happy day, her twelfth birthday. And when she comes back to live that one day again, Emily sees everything and everyone around her with extra acuity. She sees as she had never seen before.

In a recent production of the play, they conveyed this by having a very plain set for much of the play — just a few empty tables and simple chairs. No props. But for this scene, when Emily returns for her twelfth birthday, a curtain lifted on part of the stage to reveal a fully equipped kitchen, with bacon cooking on the stove. In the audience you could smell the bacon. It was as if, in that moment, we, along with Emily, could finally see.

As that scene unfolds, Emily chats with her mother while she cooks breakfast, but she becomes frustrated because her mother doesn't look at her. To Emily, from the vantage point of death, every gesture and word is significant and something to savor. To her mother, it's just another day. Emily says, "Oh Mama, just look at me as if you really saw me."

Then Emily turns to the Stage Manager and says, "I can't. I can't go on. It goes so fast. We don't have time to look at one another."

She goes on, speaking so only the Stage Manager can hear: "I didn't realize. So all that was going on and we never noticed. Take me back — up the hill — to my grave. But first: Wait! One more look. Good-bye, Good-bye world. Good-bye, Grover's Corners . . . Mama and Papa. Good-bye to clocks ticking . . . and Mama's sunflowers. And food and coffee. And new ironed dresses and hot baths . . . and sleeping and waking up. Oh earth, you're too wonderful for anyone to realize you."

Then Emily asks the Stage Manager abruptly, "Do any human beings ever realize life while they live it? — every, every minute?"

And the Stage Manager replies, "No. The saints and poets, maybe — they do some."[2]

Well, I'm not a poet, and I'm certainly not a saint. I haven't learned how to realize life while I live it, every, every minute. But there are moments, and there are glimpses — usually not more than that — when we can see something like the vision of the saints and take in the world with the eye of a poet. Most often it happens, as it did with Emily, when we've been given a fleeting chance to look back. It's revelation in retrospect. It's when we look back that we can see that, in Jacob's words, "the LORD was in this place all along, and I did not know it," that our hearts burned on the road to Emmaus, that life itself is a blessing in ways that would surely overwhelm us if we saw, really saw it, every moment of our lives.

I think the reason that the saints and poets can see this more clearly than most is that they're the only ones who can do so and not be overwhelmed. For the rest of us, those moments and glimpses will have to suffice, and they're enough to remind us that God's blessings are more extravagant than we can possibly absorb, that even as we largely skim over the surface of life, God is at work in the deeper regions.

2. Thornton Wilder, *Our Town* (New York: Harper, 1957), p. 100.

CALLED AND RECALLED

1 Corinthians 1:1-9

THERE'S AN OLD HEBREW TALE of a rabbi living in a Russian city a century ago. Disappointed by his lack of direction and purpose, he wandered out into the chilly evening. With his hands in his pockets, he aimlessly walked through the empty streets, questioning his faith in God and his calling as a rabbi. He was so enshrouded by his own despair that he mistakenly wandered into a Russian military compound that was off-limits to civilians.

The evening chill was shattered by the bark of a Russian soldier. "Who are you? And what are you doing here?"

"Excuse me?" replied the rabbi.

"I said, 'Who are you and what are you doing here?'"

After a brief moment the rabbi, in a gracious tone so as not to provoke the soldier, asked, "How much do you get paid every day?"

The soldier responded, "What does that have to do with you?"

The rabbi said, "I will pay you that same sum if you will ask me those same two questions every day: Who are you? and What are you doing here?"[1]

---

1. Wayne Cordeiro, *Doing Church as a Team* (Ventura, Calif.: Regal Books, 2001), pp. 32-33.

Of course, those two questions are questions about vocation, about calling (the two words have the same root and mean essentially the same thing): "Who are you? And what are you doing here?" If we can answer those questions, we will know both who we were created to be and what we were created to do. As the rabbi knew, it's worth a great deal to be reminded that these are *the* questions, the kind we need to keep before us continually.

These are different questions from those that usually are asked of twenty-first-century Americans. Young people are asked, "What do you want to be when you grow up?" It is often assumed that, as adults, we are to ask ourselves, "What do I want to do next?" It is the language of decision, of choice.

But if God has something particular in mind for each one of us, then different questions apply, questions that are less about what we want and more about what God has in mind. When life is approached in this way, suddenly the language of autonomous choice doesn't always apply. We begin to sense that our job is less to make choices than it is to discern what, in some sense, has already been chosen for us.

That is one reason why some people discover their vocation in childhood. I have loved learning the remarkable story of a fourteen-year-old girl name Emma Bancroft who lived on a farm in rural Michigan. The year was 1892. She made an appointment with her Presbyterian minister to tell him that she felt called to be a minister herself. He replied, "I'm so sorry, Emma, but you must be mistaken because, you see, God doesn't call women into the ministry." (At that time, very few denominations did.)

Later that week, Emma's father paid a call on the minister and said, "If Emma says she's called to preach, she's called to preach. What's more, I'm sure she could preach circles around any boy in this county!"

Emma, who by all accounts was a painfully shy young

person, was so convicted in her call that she went in search of a denomination that would ordain her. Sure enough, ten years later, in 1902, she was ordained by the Christian Church, a predecessor denomination of the United Church of Christ. But I wonder what would have happened to Emma Bancroft — who, by the way, is my grandmother; my middle name is Bancroft — if she had not had my great-grandfather.

Sometimes the voices of others can help us discern God's call, while other times they can send us in another direction entirely.

Someone once shared with me a particularly powerful memory of something that happened when he was attending summer church camp as a child. At the closing campfire, the pastor who served as chaplain of the camp suggested that perhaps during the course of their time together some of the campers may have heard God's call to service. Those who had were invited to come forward and to say a word to the pastor.

One boy approached the pastor and whispered in his ear. The pastor announced that "Michael" (or whatever his name was) had heard the call to become a parish minister. The pastor shook his hand vigorously and said, "Congratulations, Michael!"

A girl came forward next. She whispered something to the pastor, and then the pastor reported to the gathering, "Susie has heard the call to be a medical missionary. Congratulations, Susie!"

Then, when the pastor asked if anyone else had heard God's call, another boy came forward. He, too, whispered in the pastor's ear. The pastor responded by patting the boy on the shoulder. Then the boy sat down without another word being said. The person telling me this story was that boy, now a middle-aged man, a highly successful business executive. There was still some hurt in his voice when he asked, "Can you guess what I whispered in the pastor's ear? I told him that I felt called to teach mathematics."

Even as I relate that story, I get mad at that pastor all over again. And I feel sad for that boy who didn't have his sense of call confirmed. The pastor at that camp reflected a common misconception. God doesn't only call pastors and medical missionaries and the like. God also calls math teachers, carpenters, quilters, mothers, roofers, soccer coaches, soup kitchen volunteers, and gardeners.

In the very first words of his letter to the Corinthians, Paul affirms his own call: "Paul, called by the will of God to be an apostle." Those are the very first words of the letter. Obviously, Paul takes some satisfaction in his own particular call. But then, in the very next verse, he affirms that everyone reading that letter has a call — to be a saint, which in this context does not mean a canonized saint or even an especially good person. Being a saint means to be God's person in the world. And we are all called to be saints of that kind.

Novelist Frederick Buechner gives a compelling definition of vocation: "God calls us to the place where our deep gladness and the world's deep hunger meet." I might put much the same idea in a slightly different way: "We are called to the intersection of the world's great needs and our own particular gifts."

Every Christian has a vocation, a calling, an invitation to use his or her gifts in a variety of ways to meet great needs. People are in need of care and healing, so God calls some to be nurses and doctors. The world is a dangerous place, so God calls others to be lifeguards and firefighters. We are meant to live joyfully, so God calls sluggers like David Ortiz and musicians like Louis Armstrong.

And God has called you to something. Your vocation may or may not be your day job. But it's something that has your name on it. Wherever your particular gifts intersect with the world's great needs — that is the place to which God calls you. That is your vocation.

Our daughter, Alanna, has always had a compassionate heart which, from an early age, became manifest, in part, in her strong commitment to social justice. When she graduated from college, she moved to Washington, D.C., and worked with several social service organizations. She wasn't sure what was next for her, but she loved living and working in that setting.

About two years into her time there, my wife, Karen, and I received a phone call from Karen's father. He is a particularly attentive grandfather to his many grandchildren. He started out by saying, "You know, I've been thinking a lot about Alanna these days" — nothing unusual there, but then he continued — ". . . and I think she ought to consider becoming a minister."

Whoa. I didn't see that coming.

To understand the significance of that statement coming from my father-in-law, you must know that he's never been a churchgoer. In fact, he has many questions about organized religion, and he had been quite concerned about his daughter marrying a minister. In other words, this idea was coming from a most unlikely source.

So I said, "Would you call her and tell her that?"

"Sure, I'll call her right now."

About an hour later, we got a call from Alanna. "I just got off the phone with Pop-Pop."

"Oh . . ."

"Do you know what he said to me?"

"What did he say?"

"He said he thought I should become a minister!"

"Well, what do you think?"

"I think I've been waiting my whole life for someone to tell me that."

A few years later, Alanna graduated from Yale Divinity School and now serves Memorial Church at Harvard. Who knew? (Well, apparently, God and at least one other person knew right well.)

Danish philosopher Søren Kierkegaard said that each one of us is born as if with sealed orders. Our orders have our name on them, but we cannot see the contents. It is our life-long task to figure out what those orders are, even as they remain sealed. It is a lifelong task because we are not only called once, but continually. We can be called to different tasks and different roles at different times.

Clearly this was the case with Diann Bailey. She had been a pediatric nurse for twenty-seven years, the last sixteen years at Connecticut Children's Medical Center. She took great satisfaction in that work, but she also felt tugged in another direction. Diann sensed that she was called to serve others in a different way — as a pastor. So she enrolled at Andover Newton Theological School. When she graduated, she didn't yet have a call to a church. But she took the bold step of giving three months' notice at the hospital anyway. During those months Diann did some guest preaching on the side. Late in the summer, after her graduation, she was working her very last scheduled day at Children's Medical Center. It was a Thursday. With just two hours left in her final shift, she got a call from the church where she was scheduled to preach that Sunday.

The person on the other end of the phone was frantic. A one-year-old in the congregation was very ill and had been rushed to Children's Medical Center. "I know you're only our guest preacher, but, as you know, our pastor is out of the country. Could you go visit the family at Children's? I can tell you where it is. It's not too far."

Diann said, "Well, actually, I do know where it is. I'm already there." (The folks in the church didn't know that Diann was a nurse at Children's. They just knew that she was a seminary graduate and that she was preaching in their church the next Sunday.)

So Diann finished her shift and went to the nurses' station to hand in her badge and parking pass. Then she went immediately to another office to pick up her new clergy badge and called on the family — not as a nurse, as she had for so many years, but as a pastor.

I asked Diann what that was like, to be called into such immediate service, with such a quick turnaround between her role as a nurse and her role as a pastor. "I felt calm and confident," she told me. "This is what I had been training for. This is what I had now been called to do."

Just a couple of months later, Diann was ordained as the pastor of a congregation in the United Church of Christ, a confirmation — as if she needed one — of this new call in her life.

At Andover Newton Theological School, where I now serve as president, we help adults of all ages find their way to that intersection, the blessed juncture, of their particular gifts and the world's great needs.

Some are responding to an unassailable sense of call from an early age — like my grandmother, Emma Bancroft.

Others come exploring a sense of call that is still in formation — like our daughter, Alanna, did. In some way they're still seeking a clear answer to the two essential questions: "Who are you? And what are you doing here?"

Still others are in midlife, sensing that God is calling them in a new direction — like Diann Bailey.

And there are even those like the gentleman who, as a boy, sensed he was called to teach mathematics, ended up a businessman, and became a devoted Christian and lay leader, one of the ones that Paul called a saint — someone who does God's work in the world, with or without a title.

Helping people find and enter into their unique call is both a joy and a privilege. After all, as a wise person once said, the two most important days of your life are the day you're born, and the day you discover why you were born.

TO BLESS AND
TO BE BLESSED

Numbers 6:22-27

THESE DAYS THE WORD BLESS IS USED so often and in such a wide variety of contexts — many of them trivial — that the whole notion of offering a blessing is in some danger of being cheapened. We say "Bless you" when someone sneezes. Some people use the phrase "Bless you" as a substitute for "Thank you." Every president in my memory has ended speeches with the benediction ". . . and God bless America." If we ever stopped to count our blessings, we would see that there's a whole lot of blessing going on.

This isn't anything new. In the Bible, sometimes the word *bless* is used in ways that are almost perfunctory. In Hebrew scripture there are places where "The Lord bless you" is nothing more than a simple greeting, like saying "Hello."

Nevertheless, the Bible also attests to the power in this ancient act of blessing. In the creation account in the first chapter of Genesis, the Creator blesses the creatures — the birds, the fish, the animals, the human creature — and it is as if the blessing is what animates them with life. They live — we live — only through God's continued blessing.

Later in Genesis, Jacob tricked his blind father, Isaac, into giving him the blessing that was intended for his brother, Esau. Once the blessing was offered, it had such power that it couldn't be taken back and given to the one for whom it was originally intended. Esau was so furious at being cheated of his father's blessing that he decided to kill his brother. Such is the power of a blessing conferred and a blessing denied.

When Jesus was baptized, God offered this blessing: "You are my Son, the Beloved; my favor rests on you." And all his life long this blessing sustained Jesus; he nestled in it, wrapped himself in it. We might even say that this blessing equipped Jesus to face all that he had to face and empowered him to do all that he was able to do.

Perhaps the most familiar benediction of all is found in the book of Numbers: "The LORD bless you and keep you: The LORD make his face to shine upon you, and be gracious unto you: The LORD lift up his countenance upon you, and give you peace" (Num. 6:24-26). That blessing is considered so powerful that it is introduced with the instruction that only priests are to bless — as if to say that offering a blessing is such serious business that it is best left to the professionals.

I can add my own witness to the power of blessing. In the context of worship, when it's time for a blessing to be offered, I can feel it in the room. There's a heightened sense of attention. I get the feeling that fewer people are compiling shopping lists in their minds or wondering if they left the iron on. Clearly, something is happening here, something that demands attention. People don't want to miss it.

When a child is baptized, the pastor says, "I baptize you in the name of the Father, and of the Son, and of the Holy Spirit, one God and mother of us all. The Holy Spirit be upon you, child of God, disciple of Christ, member of Christ's church. You are marked with the sign of the cross forever." Those are words of blessing, of course, and you can tell the words have power because they never sound old; it's almost as if we lean forward to hear them for the first time. In the same way, when someone is ordained or commissioned with the laying on of hands and a prayer of blessing — it is always an electric moment.

The benediction offered at the conclusion of a worship service is a simple act, just a sentence or two of good words — which is what *benediction* means, "good words" — but that one moment seems to gather up all of the sacred energy in the room, as if we all long to be wrapped in a blessing before we leave to face the world outside, as if we know that somehow this ancient act addresses a timeless need for God's blessing to be heard, to be received.

My friend Tony Robinson says that since he retired from being a pastor, the pastoral duty he misses most is the opportunity to bless people. He writes, "I throw my arms up in the air, as if embracing God's flock, and then utter a good word, a benediction. It seems vaguely superstitious and ancient; on the one hand, maybe a little threatening, and yet on the other hand, hopeful and promising, and quite loving."[1]

The narrator of Marilynne Robinson's Pulitzer Prize–winning novel, *Gilead,* is Pastor Ames, who is writing to his young son. In one passage he describes his sense of gratitude that as a pastor he is so often the one who offers blessings. He goes on to assure his son that a person does not "have to be a minister to confer blessing. You are simply much more likely to find yourself in that position. It's a thing people expect of you."[2]

By affirming that anyone can offer a blessing, Ames reveals that he is a Protestant pastor and not a priest in the ancient tabernacle. In a blessing we are invoking God's life-giving Spirit, and because we believe that Spirit is available to all, anyone can offer a blessing. It isn't just for the professionals. The power in the blessing is not ours; we only borrow it from

1. Anthony B. Robinson, *Common Grace* (Seattle: Sasquatch Books, 2006), p. 78.

2. Marilynne Robinson, *Gilead* (New York: Farrar, Straus & Giroux, 2004), p. 23.

God. We invoke it. We channel it. The words have power because they are carried on the wings of God's Holy Spirit. We are merely the messengers, not the source, of blessing. The gift of blessing is one we pass on from the God from whom all blessings flow.

When the psalmist says, "Bless the LORD, O my soul," it can sound as if we're doing the blessing on our own, as if the tables are turned and we're blessing God. But we have no power to bless apart from God. To bless God, then, is to give back to God something of the blessing we have received from God. It's not something we do on our own. When we bless God, it is by taking our part in the endless echo of grace.

If there is great power in the act of blessing, why don't we offer more blessings to one another?

One reason is that we may assume that the people we care about don't need a blessing. We think our children need advice. We see that our parents need support. A friend needs a listening ear. Someone home from the hospital needs a meal delivered. A spouse needs a kind word. Much of the time we can sense what the people around us need, but we rarely consider that what that person may need more than anything else, what that person may be hungry for — in some cases dying of hunger for — is a blessing.

The late Henri Nouwen wisely wrote, "To bless means to say good things. We have to bless one another constantly. Parents need to bless their children, children their parents, husbands their wives, wives their husbands, friends their friends. . . . Whether the blessing is given in words or in gestures, in a solemn or an informal way, our lives need to be blessed lives."[3]

Nouwen's words have the quality of a reminder because I

3. Henri Nouwen, *Bread for the Journey* (San Francisco: HarperOne, 1997), September 7 entry.

think we know that there's power in blessing. We just forget. I know of men and women — and you do too — who have waited their whole lives long to receive a blessing from a father or a mother. I know of parents — and you do too — who would get on the next plane and fly across the country if they thought they might receive their child's blessing. And it's the same for spouses and partners and friends.

Tony Robinson recalls one particularly significant act of blessing in his own life:

> I remember how long I waited before receiving a blessing from my father, who had Alzheimer's disease. During his last three years he lived in a small facility with twenty others in various stages of the disease. The summer before he died, my [wife and I] were there for a visit. The three of us were walking together arm in arm, my wife and I on either side of him. We moved at his slow pace across the dining room toward the door, which led to an enclosed garden. By this time my dad seldom said much that made sense to us. Even his words had become difficult to understand, his speech often slurred. As we crossed the dining room his slippered shuffle drew to a halt. Bent over, he looked up at me and clear as a bell said, "You are a good man." Then he resumed his shuffle toward the door. My wife said, "Did you hear that?" She did not mean, "Did you hear the words he said?" She meant, "Did you hear, really hear, what he was saying to you?" It was my father's blessing. Three months later he died.[4]

Henri Nouwen was right: "We have to bless one another constantly."

I know of a mother who, the last thing before sending her children off to school, would put her hand on the head

4. Anthony B. Robinson, *Common Grace*, pp. 142-43.

of each. And she would say silently to herself, *Bless you and keep you.* It reached the point that if one of her children left the house without that gesture of blessing, she would come back for it, as if it were as essential as lunch money — and, of course, in a sense it is. A blessing can feed a kind of hunger, a hunger of which we may be only dimly aware, but which is very real and sometimes very deep.

When our son, Todd, was a boy, he would often wake up in the morning with what we called "bed-head" (what other people call "a bad hair day"). I would take some water in my hand to smooth a cowlick and say as I did, "I baptize you in the name of the Father, and of the Son, and of the Holy Spirit." Usually I said it in a light-hearted manner, as if it were only another of our shared jokes. But, to me, it was also a wonderful moment in the day as I remembered the day when I slathered his hair with the waters of baptism. In other words, that daily ritual was a chance to bless this child of mine. And we all need a blessing. There are blessings we need to give and blessings we need to receive.

The other reason we may not offer a blessing is that we've concluded that someone doesn't deserve a blessing.

Someone shared with me this wonderful Gaelic blessing: "May those who love us, love us. And those who don't love us, may God turn their hearts; and if he doesn't turn their hearts, may he turn their ankles, so we'll know them by their limping." Doesn't that capture the kind of blessing that we're sometimes tempted to offer? It's more like a curse — which, of course, is the opposite of a blessing. Sometimes the good words stick on our tongues.

In a radio interview, Lee Smith, a wonderful Southern novelist, pointed out that, in the South, you can say anything about someone that might be thought of as critical or unkind — as long as you add the phrase "Bless her heart" or "Bless his heart." "She's such a vain and self-centered woman, bless her heart." "He's an ungrateful little man, bless his heart." It's a quirky manner of speech, but I also think it's more than that, something quite profound, actually. To say "Bless her heart" is to ask God to do something we find difficult — perhaps even impossible — to do ourselves. We're asking God to bless because we have no good words to offer ourselves.

As I've said, words of blessing are borrowed words. We're asking God to bless because we may not have any good words of our own to offer. It's similar to the dynamic in asking God to forgive someone. Sometimes we ask God to forgive someone because we know that, at this moment at least, we're not yet ready to forgive. So Jesus on the cross did not say "I forgive you" but rather "Father, forgive them" — God forgive them — "for they know not what they do." To say "May God forgive you" or "May God bless you" is to borrow the power of God to forgive or to offer good words, words of blessing, when that seems beyond us. It is asking God to take the lead. It is asking God to work through us, even though we are such flawed instruments.

We see this dynamic at work in Marilynne Robinson's wonderful novel *Gilead*. Much of the latter half of it is an account of Pastor Ames's struggle with what is expected of him in relation to his namesake, John Ames Boughton, or Jack, whom he would rather curse than bless. Jack is the son of Ames's best friend, and he's done many hurtful things that Ames finds hard to get past. Ames doesn't trust Jack and finds his presence unsettling, even vaguely threatening. When Jack begins to confess some of the things he's done while he was away from home, the old pastor struggles to listen with a compassionate ear, his soul torn between his feelings of dislike and the obligations of his vocation.

As Jack prepares to leave town again, Ames says to him, "The thing I would like, actually, is to bless you." Jack is surprised by the request. Perhaps Ames is surprised too. But if you're a pastor, it is what you do. You get to offer blessings. Sometimes you have to offer blessings. Ames writes to his son, "Well, anyway, I told him it was an honor to bless him. And that was absolutely true. In fact I'd have gone through seminary and ordination and all the years intervening for that one moment." Before Jack departs, Ames says to him, "We all love you, you know."[5]

Sometimes we are given a privileged glimpse of the holy mystery of God's grace, not because we understand it, or have any claim on it, but because for a moment at least, we have actually been a channel for it. That's what can happen when we offer blessings and other gestures of love — even to those we might find unlovable. Somehow the act of blessing and being blessed puts us in a place where God is apt to draw near and sometimes, through blessing and being blessed, we can find that love, or something very much like it, has taken up residence in our hearts. When the presence of God touches such a moment, both the one blessed and the one offering the blessing are given a gift.

5. Marilynne Robinson, *Gilead*, pp. 241-42.

THE CLOUD OF WITNESSES

Hebrews 12:1-2

FTER I WAS CALLED AS Senior Minister of First Congregational Church in Burlington, Vermont, I was given a tour of the building by a church member. When we got to the formal church parlor, I paused to take in the portraits of my predecessors hanging on the walls. With something like awe, I said, "There they are. The cloud of witnesses." I was only twenty-seven years old at the time, in many ways too young to know that I was too young to be taking on this job. But even then I knew that I would need all the help I could get to run my leg of the race.

Soon thereafter, and every Wednesday morning for nine years, I led a Bible study in that room. The group who gathered, made up largely of women in their seventies and eighties, had been meeting there each week for longer than they could remember, which meant, for some of them, since before I was born. We used the format they had been using for all those years. We would read the Bible passages to be used in worship that week, and then we would pray together.

At first I prepared my lessons with meticulous care, brandishing all of the historical-critical methods of scholarship I had learned in seminary. There was so much that I wanted to communicate. The women in the class listened with what seemed to be genuine interest as I demonstrated my academic acumen. They would ask follow-up questions, which I took to be something like asking for an encore performance.

Over time, however, the focus and tenor of the class began to change. The members of the class began gently to redirect the conversation to the ways in which the Bible passages were speaking to what was going on in their lives. They also began to bring in what was going on in the congregation and in the world and seeking to know what the Bible might say about that. When it came time for offering prayer requests, I would often learn more about what was going on in the lives of my parishioners than I would in any other way. They were lovingly brooding over the congregation with their prayers, as well as over their young minister, who was still learning his way around the congregation.

During my first winter there, the first big snow storm happened on a Wednesday morning. I couldn't get out of my driveway. Not yet accustomed to life in Vermont, I was a bit surprised that, when I called the church office, someone was there to answer the phone. I said, "Quite a storm, isn't it? Obviously, we won't be having Bible study today." The person on the other end of the line replied, "Well, I'll go tell the ladies. . . . They'll be so disappointed." Sure enough, they were all there, with Bibles open, waiting dutifully for their new young minister, who didn't even know how to get out of his own driveway. They never teased me about that directly, but conversation did turn to weather conditions with suspicious frequency after that.

One day I gave the class a dissertation on the need to move beyond exclusively male language in reference to God. I thought I was introducing a potentially radical concept to the group. The next week one member quietly sought me out before class. She had a book of prayers she wanted to show me. It had been given to her by her mother some seventy years earlier. She had marked several passages that referred to God using female imagery, as Mother as well as Father. Without a hint of reprimand, but more to share a sense of wonder, she said, "There really is nothing new under the sun."

Through the years I came to look forward to those classes as an opportunity to teach, to be sure, but even more as a chance to learn. During one class, in response to a hurtful episode that required her to forgive, Thelma Connor said, "I have taken the whole episode, thrown it in the deepest part of the pond, and put up a sign that says, 'No fishing!'" That remains one of the best descriptions of forgiveness I know. Thelma Norton, when she was about to say something critical of a fellow church member, would always stop herself by saying, "Well, I'll just say 'Amen' to that," and then move on. I often invoke that phrase now myself when I'm in a similar position. And Marjorie Perrin wisely commented on the need to confront someone who was heading down a dangerous path: "When you reach my age, you realize that you don't have time to waste on anything but the truth."

But beyond any specific words of advice I received, that group helped shape me by showing me what a Christian life looks like. It is, among other things: showing up week after week, in and out of season, supporting one another in difficult times, letting prayers expand the scope of our concern, having an eye trained to spot the one in need, practicing forgiveness, staying open to whatever new thing God might be doing. Nothing dramatic, perhaps. And yet, how remarkable.

A while back I had the opportunity to return to that church after many years away. Among other things, I wanted to go to the church parlor. Not much had changed, except now my portrait hung among those of my predecessors. What I most wanted to experience in that room, however, was the continued presence of the members of that Wednesday-morning Bible study group, almost all of whom had since died. I felt a need to express my gratitude for their faithfulness and, of course, to be cheered on for my leg of the race that, unlike theirs, was not yet complete. And, sure enough, there they all were, like a cloud of witnesses, and in ways that went beyond my imagining.